Radical Christianity

Practical Principles for a Life of Power

John 13-17

Eddie Rasnake

Copyright © 2019 Eddie Rasnake
All rights reserved. No part of this book may be reproduced in any form without the expressed written consent of the copyright owner.

DEDICATION

This book is dedicated to my fellow Cru staff members at the University of Tennessee: Fawzy and Linda Attia, Carla Butler, Doug Byrd, Tad and Linda Dacus, Julia Helander, Hank and Chrissy Marshman, Jeff and Amy Pitts, Doug Pollock, and Davalyn Redford. It was a privilege to serve the Lord together with you!

Books by Eddie Rasnake:

What Should I Do, Lord?
One Another: The Community God Wants Us To Be

Working Thru The Word Series:
Colossians
Jude
James
2 Corinthians
Righteousness of the Heart (The Sermon on the Mount – Matthew 5-7)
Radical Christianity (The Upper Room Discourse – John 13-17)
Dangers to Devotion (Letters to the 7 Churches – Revelation 2-3)

Discipleship Series:
Becoming a Disciple
Becoming a Discipler
Becoming an Elder
God's Will
Transforming Truths

Following God Bible Study Series:
First Steps for the New Christian
Living God's Will
Ephesians
Romans
The Acts of the Holy Spirit 1 (1-12)
The Acts of the Holy Spirit 2 (13-28)
Using Your Spiritual Gifts
How to Develop a Quiet Time
Spiritual Warfare

Following God: Co-Authored with Wayne Barber and Rick Shepherd
Women of the Bible – Book 1
Women of the Bible – Book 2
Life Principles from the Old Testament
Kings of the Old Testament
Prophets of the Old Testament
Men of the New Testament
Life Principles for Worship from the Tabernacle

Co-Authored with Michele Rasnake
Held in His Grace: A Young Mother's Journey Through Cancer

CONTENTS

	Acknowledgments	i
1	Radical Christians live by a Radical Principle (13:1-38)	1
2	Radical Christians Understand a Radical Promise (14:1-7)	12
3	Radical Christians live by a Radical Power (14:8-31)	29
4	Radical Christians have a Radical Purpose (15:1-17)	42
5	Radical Christians have a Radical Potential (15:18-16:15)	54
6	Radical Christians face a Radical Prospect (16:16-33)	65
7	Radical Christians are a result of a Radical Prayer (17:1-26)	76

Introduction

__Background Assignment__

Read John 13-17 through in one sitting at least three different times using several different translations of the Bible. What do you see as the "Big Idea" of this passage - your theme?

*Author's Note - Although there are many fine translations of the Bible, for studying purposes I would recommend the New American Standard Version or the Christian Standard Version. The method of translation (word for word) with these versions is perhaps not as easy to read as the New International Version (which is translated phrase for phrase), but is more technically exact for Bible study. It is recent enough as well to have made use of the more contemporary discoveries of manuscripts, which allows it to be more accurate than the King James version. Because the study questions are written to use with the NASB, you may need to reference it if you have difficulty because of using another version.

Background

The Author

The gospel of John was authored by the apostle John, who wrote more books in the New Testament than anyone else except Paul. Scholars used to insist (wrongly) that it was not written until the second century and therefore couldn't have been written by John. However, the "Rylands" papyrus fragment, dated around 135 A.D., contains portions of chapter 18. That discovery makes a 2nd century date impossible. More time would be needed between the occasion of writing and its circulation as far as Egypt, where the papyrus was written. John was the only one of Christ's disciples who it is believed did not die a martyr's death, although one tradition holds that he was boiled in oil but wouldn't die. Although John is credited as the author, the bulk of the passage we are studying is John quoting Jesus Christ directly.

The younger brother of James of the family of Zebedee, John apparently came from a fairly well-to-do home. Along with his brother he held the nickname "sons of thunder" (Mark 3:17). John had a unique relationship with Christ. He was one of three key disciples who were with Christ virtually all the time during His public ministry (along with Peter and James - see Matthew 26:37 and Mark 9:2, etc.). He was called the "beloved disciple" (John 13:23, 20:2, and 21:7,20) and on the cross Christ gave John the responsibility of caring for Mary, His mother (John 19:25-27).

The Audience

...OF CHRIST – Christ is addressing these words directly to the twelve disciples (although Judas missed most of it). The context is the Passover feast just prior to the crucifixion and the discourse begins in the upper room where Christ washes their feet and institutes the sacrament of communion. It then continues on the walk from the upper room to Gethsemane on the Mount of Olives.

...OF JOHN – John compiles his account of the life of Christ including a selection of key snapshots with the expressed purpose of encouraging the reader to believe. John is writing to a general audience of his day as well as being particularly applicable to ours. The applications from this section specifically are aimed not just at encouraging our faith but at facilitating a growing faith.

The Aim

...OF CHRIST – Christ's main purpose in sharing what He does here seems to be to prepare the disciples for His eminent departure (John 13:1), to prevent them from anxiety about this (14:1), and to keep them from stumbling (16:1).

...OF JOHN – John's reason for communicating the truths of these chapters, as well as the rest of the book, is expressed in John 20:31, "...these have been written that you may believe that Jesus is the Christ, the Son of God; and that believing you may have life in His name." This is by far the most theological of all the gospels, with special emphasis on the deity of Christ.

LESSON ONE

"Radical Christians Live By a Radical Principle"

John 13:1-38

The Illustration Of Attitude (13:1-11)

📖 What is the "Feast of Passover", and what is the context of Christ's discourse here?

The feast of Passover was inaugurated by Moses just prior to Pharaoh's release of Israel (Exodus 34). The angel of death was to kill the first-born of everyone, and by observing God's commands for Israel, their houses were "passed over." It became an annual feast in Israel as a reminder of God's past deliverance, and as a tutor of His future deliverance from our sins through Christ. In 1 Corinthians 5:7 Paul calls Christ "our Passover." It is no coincidence that Christ, our Passover lamb, was sacrificed during the observance of the Passover week. The context of Christ's discourse here, according to John 13:1 is a) Passover week, and b) Christ's "hour" (meaning the fulfillment of His purpose on earth).

📖 Identify the references to love in verse 1 and how the truth of verse 2 relates to it.

RADICAL CHRISTIANITY

Verse 1 teaches us that not only had Christ loved the disciples, but also that He kept loving them to the end. The word "love" here is AGAPE, meaning unconditional love. We see from the rest of John's gospel that Christ expressed this love for the disciples by a) washing their feet, b) teaching them this "Upper Room Discourse", c) by praying for them (chapter 17), and d) by dying for them. Verse 2 reminds us that Judas already planned to betray the Lord, and Jesus knew this, yet He washed his feet. Jesus also knew that in a matter of hours all of His disciples would abandon Him, and that Peter would deny Him three times. The actions of our Lord this night are truly unconditional.

📖 Look at verses 3-5 writing your observations on how these relate to the theme of unconditional love.

Verse 3 shows us that Jesus knew and understood His place in God's plan. He was to rule and reign over all creation, and yet we see Him wash the disciples' feet. You know, most of us don't mind being called a servant, we just don't want to be treated like one. Yet here we see the Lord Himself taking the role of a servant.

📖 What is the cultural background of "washing feet", and who would normally do it?

Palestine is a very dry, dusty land, and at the time of Christ, the common method of transportation was walking. Even traveling a short distance resulted in dirty feet, so it was customary for a host to provide for the feet of his guests to be washed. Normally this duty fell on a slave. It was a humble job with no glory.

PRACTICAL PRINCIPLES FOR A LIFE OF POWER

📖 What are your observations on Peter's comments and what is the meaning of Christ's response in verse 10?

In Peter's comment, "Lord, do You wash my feet?", the word "You" appears as an "Emphatic Personal Pronoun." In other words, Peter is saying, "Lord, do YOU wash my feet?". Peter has a right heart, but a wrong perspective. He doesn't understand the point of what Jesus is doing. Jesus' answer is, "Later you will understand." Peter is confused and says "NEVER!." This word is an "Emphatic Future Negative" meaning "not now, not ever." It uses the stronger Greek word for the negative (*ou*). Peter isn't taking Jesus at His word. Jesus says, "If I don't wash you, you have no part with Me."

There is a symbolism here that is lost on Peter. Jesus isn't just talking about physical dirt, but washing away sins. Peter is still out to lunch, and now says, "wash my hands and my head too." Jesus replies, "If you have already been cleansed (bathed) then washing the feet is enough." To understand this we must look back to the culture. Someone who took a bath before they left their house would not need another one upon arrival. Washing the feet would be enough. There is a spiritual parallel here. It seems Jesus is contrasting initial forgiveness of our sins with confession of new sins afterward. Once we are saved, we don't ever need to be justified all over again (take a spiritual bath), we merely need to deal with the filth we pick up along the way (confess sins as they happen). This is the point of verse 10.

📖 What does verse 11 indicate about the state of Judas' spirituality?

From this verse, and the preceding statement at the end of verse 10, we can infer that Judas was not a believer. It wasn't his betrayal that kept him out of heaven, but his unbelief. His betrayal, though wrong, was not as bad as the actions of Peter who denied the Lord three times. The difference between the two lies in how they responded to their failures.

The Instruction Of Action (13:12-20)

📖 What according to verses 12-16 is the object lesson of Christ's actions?

In these verses we see that Christ's washing of the disciples' feet was not an end in itself, but served as an object lesson in humility. His points are: a) If I (the greater) can do this, then you (the lessor) can as well, b) I did this as an example, and c) Not to follow My example is to exalt yourself above Me. Since the illustration has to do with forgiveness, the primary application lies in this direction. In other words, "since I forgive you, you must forgive one another."

📖 Should the exhortation of verse 14 be taken literally or figuratively, and what are some of the practical ways we can apply this principle today?

Obviously, Jesus' point is not for us to wash each other's feet today. It was a culturally relevant illustration that is not relevant to today's culture. We don't get our feet dirty from walking. Take a few moments to let the group brainstorm on some practical ways this principle can be applied today.

📖 Break verse 17 down into it's essential components and write your observations.

There are two essential components here. First, we need to "know" (to perceive with the sense) this principle Jesus is discussing. Then we must "do" it. Knowing alone is not enough. Jesus makes it clear that the blessing comes not from knowing only, but from doing what we know (obedience). James teaches "prove yourselves doers of the word and not merely hearers who delude themselves." His point is, knowledge without application becomes a deluding influence. It deceives us into thinking that we are spiritual because of what we know instead of what we live. In Luke 6:46 Jesus says, "Why do you call me Lord, Lord, and do not do what I say?" Saying He is Lord is worthless if we do not live accordingly.

📖 Where does the quote in verse 18 come from and how does it relate here?

The statement in verse 18 is a quote from Psalm 41:9, a messianic prophecy which reads, "Even my close friend, in whom I trusted, who ate my bread, has lifted up his heel against me." He is, of course, referring to Judas, and from our vantage point it is easy to see that even by the shared morsel of verse 26, Judas is implicated.

📖 Using cross-references find out what you can about the phrase "I AM HE" (literally, "I AM") and write your observations on its meaning here.

In Exodus 3:14 God answers Moses' question about His name by saying "I AM WHO I AM." When Jesus uses the term "I AM" He is making Himself equal with God. What He is saying here is, "I am going to tell you what is going to happen before it happens so that you will believe that I am God." Verse 18 is an example of Christ's foreknowledge. Remember, John is writing his gospel so that we might believe, so he is showing the things that caused him to believe.

📖 Identify each of the different people spoken of in verse 20 and the message of the verse.

There are three people here: a) The one sent by Jesus (all who carry the gospel message to unbelievers), b) The Lord Jesus, who sends them, and c) God the Father who sent the Lord Jesus. The message here is accepting the gospel bearer (listening to his message) means accepting Christ, which means accepting the Father. Rejecting the gospel bearer means rejecting Christ which means rejecting the Father.

The Incident Of Application (13:21-38)

📖 Read the parallel passage of Matthew 26:17-56 and write any observations.

The observations that can be made are innumerable. When studying a passage from one of the gospels it is always helpful to look at see if there are other accounts in order to get a fuller picture of the events you are studying.

📖 What do you think it means that Jesus was "troubled in spirit", and how does this relate to the one spoken of in verse 21?

Here we see the human side of our Lord. The one spoken of here is obviously Judas, and the knowledge of Judas' betrayal is troublesome to Jesus. Jesus felt all of the same emotions you and I feel, but He never let them become an impetus to sin. We see from Matthew's account that the disciples were "deeply grieved" by this news.

📖 Using cross-references identify the disciple spoken of in verse 21.

Cross-referencing should have led you to verse 26 where Jesus discloses to John exactly to whom He refers: Judas. Luke 22:21-22 adds the additional pronouncement from Jesus: "For indeed, the Son of Man is going as it has been determined, but woe to that man by whom He is betrayed!" Matthew 26:23-24 goes even further and adds, "It would have been good for that man if he had not been born."

📖 What is the cultural significance of Christ "dipping the morsel" and handing it to Judas, and what does this reflect about Christ?

At meals in this part of the world it was customary for the host to offer one of the guests a morsel of bread as a gesture of special friendship. Jesus was communicating unconditional love for Judas.

📖 What does the word "glorify" mean as it is used in verses 31-33?

The term "glorify" means "to bring honor." In the writings of John, the glory of God is the revelation and manifestation of all that He has and is. It is His revelation in which He manifests all the goodness that He is (John 12:28). Since Christ made this manifest, He is said to glorify the Father (John 17:1,4), or the Father is glorified in Him (John 13:31; 14:13). When Christ is said to be glorified, it means simply that His innate glory is brought to light, made manifest.

📖 Write your observations on Christ's "new commandment" and identify the results of obeying it.

The significance of Christ returning to heaven is that there will now be a vacuum of God's love on earth unless we allow Him to love others through us. Notice that this is a "commandment", not a suggestion. The measure of our call to love is the very love of Christ. The result of this, according to Christ, is that "all men will know that you are My disciples." True unconditional love comes only from God. When we are yielded to Him, and He produces this love in us, there is no doubt as to the source. We learn from the parallel accounts in the other gospels that at this point they sang a hymn and then left the upper room to walk to Gethsemane.

📖 Compare verses 36-38 with their parallel passages (Matthew 26:31-35, Mark 14:26-31, and Luke 22:31-34, 54-62) writing your observations, and try to identify how this relates to the context of chapter 13.

In verses 36-38 the point seems to be that "talk is cheap." Mark 14:26-31 adds "all of you will fall away" and Jesus quotes Zechariah 13:7 – "I will strike down the shepherd, and the sheep shall be scattered." In verse 31 we learn that all the disciples were saying they wouldn't fall away. In Matthew 26:31-35 we see this same message. In Luke 22:31-34, 54-62 we see the additional truth of Satan sifting Peter and Jesus praying that his faith would not fail (notice what Jesus prays and does not pray). We also see Peter's denial and bitter weeping when he realizes what he has done.

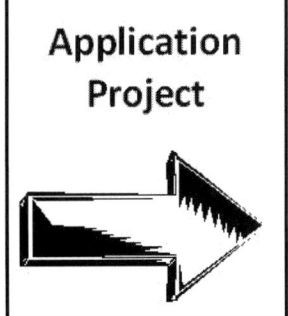

Application Project

"But I am afraid, lest as the serpent deceived Eve by his craftiness, your minds should be led astray by the simplicity and purity of devotion to Christ." - 2 Corinthians 11:3

The most radical truth in all the Scriptures and thus in all of life is that the all-powerful Creator God loves me, His rebellious creation, unreservedly, unendingly, and unconditionally. He really does. He doesn't have to, but He wants to. When it comes to radical Christianity, the one thing that controls how much I experience and live it is the degree to which I know and understand the love of God. Paul prays in Ephesians 3:19 that they might "know the love of

Christ which surpasses knowledge" and he says the result of that is being "filled up to all the fullness of God." The paradox is that whatever my comprehension is of God's love, it is inadequate and incomplete and perpetually in need of deepening. As we deepen in understanding God's love, we have a greater capacity of reflecting it to others - "we love because He first loved us" (1 John 4:19). This is what transformed John the "son of thunder" into John the "beloved disciple." Conversely, "the one who does not love does not know God, for God is love" (1 John 4:8). Consider the following applications as you pursue a more radical Christianity.

1. Identify one specific example you have seen of God's unconditional love for you.

2. What successes have you seen in your being able to love others with God's love, and what were the results?

3. What are some examples of failing to do that, and what were the results?

4. Second Timothy 3:16 states "all Scripture is inspired by God and is profitable for TEACHING, for REPROOF, for CORRECTION, and for TRAINING IN RIGHTEOUSNESS." With that as an outline, consider the following for application:

A. TEACHING: What from this passage do I need to believe?

B. REPROOF: Is there any sin I need to confess?

C. CORRECTION: What do I need to do differently?

D. TRAINING IN RIGHTEOUSNESS: What is my main application point? (make it specific and measurable)

Who is going to hold me accountable to this?

When am I going to do it? (put it in your schedule)

The most important thing in the Christian life is not what you know, but what you do with what you know (James 1:22, Luke 6:46).

Reminder:

John 14:15 states "if you love Me you will keep My commandments" and then in verses 16-17 Christ explains how we do that – ("and I will ask the Father, and He will give you another Helper...that is the Spirit..."). It is all-important that as we look at the applications God calls us to in His word, we recognize that we will only be able to accomplish those as we draw on the power of His Spirit indwelling us. Otherwise we will find ourselves trying to obey God through self-effort and we will ultimately fail. We see this necessity even in Christ. As John 14:10 puts it, "...the Father abiding in Me does His works." Why not take a moment to pray about this and give it to the Lord.

LESSON TWO

"RADICAL CHRISTIANS UNDERSTAND A RADICAL PROMISE"
John 14:1-7

The beginning of John chapter 14 is a pivotal point in the Upper Room conversation. Jesus drops the bombshell news to His disciples that He is leaving them. The seven verses we will look at in this lesson are placed in a cultural frame that is foreign to us today. Christ uses betrothal language and the process of engagement and marriage to illustrate the relationship between Him and the disciples, and ultimately between Christ and the believer. These cultural cues would have been obvious to the disciples, and in this week's lesson we will look at the verses through the eyeglasses of Biblical culture at the time of Christ, so we don't miss the larger imagery that is part of the message Jesus is communicating here.

The Betrothal

 📖 What does the word "betrothal" in 2 Corinthians 11:2 mean and what observations can you make from this verse about how this is supposed to work?

The word "betrothal" is a synonym for engagement. In the case of 2 Corinthians 11:2, Paul says "I betrothed you to one husband." Paul was the one who introduced them to their prospective bridegroom, and it was his objective that on the wedding day, the bride would still be "a pure virgin." In a practical sense, spiritual unfaithfulness to Christ is the equivalent of an engaged woman sleeping around before the wedding.

📖 What does Ephesians 5:31-32 say marriage was created to mirror, and what are the ramifications of this?

Clearly, marriage on a human level is to mirror the relationship between Christ and the church (His bride). Again, we see the clear parallel between our relationship to Christ, and the relationship of a husband and wife. The present stage of that relationship is the engagement phase.

📖 Second Corinthians 1:22 and Ephesians 1:14 relate similar things about how our engagement to Christ is formalized. Identify the meanings of the words "sealed" and "pledge", writing your observations.

The root word for "sealed" is the word for a signet ring and that it is the way it is normally used in Scripture. It paints the cultural picture of a formal document that the king would "notarize" by melting a pool of candle wax on the document and placing the impression of his signet ring in the wax to authenticate the document as well as to protect it. This same word is used of the seal placed on Jesus' tomb by the Roman soldiers. In Roman times, the perspective Paul would be writing from, the penalty for breaking such a seal without authority was death. God has guaranteed our salvation (our wedding to Christ) by sealing us with His Spirit. In order for our salvation to fail, it is not us, but the very Spirit of God who must fail. We are as secure as God Himself. The word "pledge" carries the idea of a "down payment" or "collateral" for a loan; a guarantee that you will repay or fulfill your obligation. Ephesians 1:14 teaches that the Holy Spirit in our hearts is God's guarantee of our redemption. It is interesting that this same word is used in modern Greece today as their word for an engagement ring.

The Preparation

📖 Look at John 14:1-3, identifying Christ's preparatory work for His marriage to the church.

In Jewish culture, once a couple became engaged, you entered the preparation phase. For the groom this meant "going to prepare a place for his bride" (see verse 2). Depending on the financial resources of the family, this would either be a special room in their house ("In My Father's house"), or if they were more wealthy, a separate mansion on the father's property. The engagement would last until this "dwelling place" were completed and met the approval of the father. The son wouldn't determine when the work was complete, for he would be tempted to throw up a pup tent and go get his bride. The father, being more objective, would make sure adequate provision was made for the couple's residence.

📖 What do Matthew 24:36,42 and 25:1-13 relate about the preparation needed by Israel and believers?

Israel and the church have separate, distance roles in this spiritual wedding process. The church is the bride of Christ, and Israel represents the bridesmaids. In a Jewish wedding, neither the bride nor the bridesmaids knew when the groom would come for his bride.

In fact, even the groom didn't know, but "the Father alone" knew, since he must approve their dwelling place and then he would send the son to get his bride. Because of this, the bride would prepare herself every day for her coming groom. She would put on her wedding dress and have her belongings packed and ready to go at a moment's notice. She had to "be alert" (verse 42). Likewise, Israel, represented in Matthew 25:1-13 as the "ten virgins" or bridesmaids, were called to "be alert" since they did not know "the day nor the hour." Unfortunately, not all of Israel will participate in the wedding of the lamb, but only the faithful remnant.

The Engagement (14:4-7)

📖 How according to John 14:4-7 do we become engaged to Christ?

In a very tangible sense, we who know Christ are not yet saved. A more accurate way of putting it is that we are "being saved". There are three dimensions to salvation. The first is "justification." This is what occurs immediately when I put my trust in Christ. It involves the canceling of my debt of sin, removing the penalty of my sins. The next aspect of salvation is "sanctification." This is the process of growth that began when I first met Christ and continues as long as I am on earth. It deals with the removing of the power of sin over my life. As I grow, God changes me from "glory to glory" (bit-by-bit) as He conforms me to Christ. The third part of the salvation process is called "glorification." This is the culminating, perfecting work God does at the rapture when I "become as He is" (1 John 3:2). It is the total eradication of the presence of sin in my life in preparation for eternity in the presence of God. As we look at this process in the light of John 14:4-7, our "engagement" occurs when we initially place our trust in Christ, and from that point until heaven is the engagement period. The wedding occurs in heaven.

The Coming For The Bride (Rapture)

📖 What cultural picture is painted by the Jewish wedding ceremony and how does this relate to the rapture and second coming?

In Jewish culture at the time of Christ, a wedding followed a very specific process. To a Jewish audience, any reference to engagement and marriage would be understood in that cultural context. Unless we understand that culture, we might not catch all the subtle nuances of what is being communicated in the Scriptures. In a Jewish wedding, once the engagement was formalized, the groom would work on preparing a place for the couple to live after marriage. The bride, meanwhile, would await the completion of this task and his coming for her. Once the groom had the father's approval that the dwelling place was finished, he would lead a processional from his father's house to the bride's house. As they neared the bride's house someone would run ahead and warn her with a shout or by blowing a trumpet. She and her family would come out to meet the groom and accompany him back to the father's house for seven days of celebration culminating in the wedding feast when the bride and broom would be presented. They would then take up residence in the prepared dwelling place. When you lay this cultural practice over the Biblical teaching on the rapture, the similarities are obvious. Jesus is the groom and the church is the bride. Since His ascension and the inauguration of the church age, He has been "preparing a place for us" (John 14:1-3). When that work will be finished, only the Father knows (Matthew 24:36,42; 25:13). Once it is complete, He will come for us. His coming will be announced by a shout from the archangel (Michael) and a trumpet (1 Thessalonians 4:16; 1 Cor. 15:52), and we will go out to meet Him (1 Thessalonians 4:17). We will then go to the Father's house for seven days (apparently Daniel's 70th week which is the tribulation for those who remain on earth – Daniel 9:24,27) culminating in the "marriage supper of the Lamb" (Revelation 19:9), and the presentation of the church, His bride, at the 2nd coming (Revelation 19:8,14). As you can see, only a "pre-tribulation rapture" fits the cultural context that the New Testament writers and readers would have been operating from.

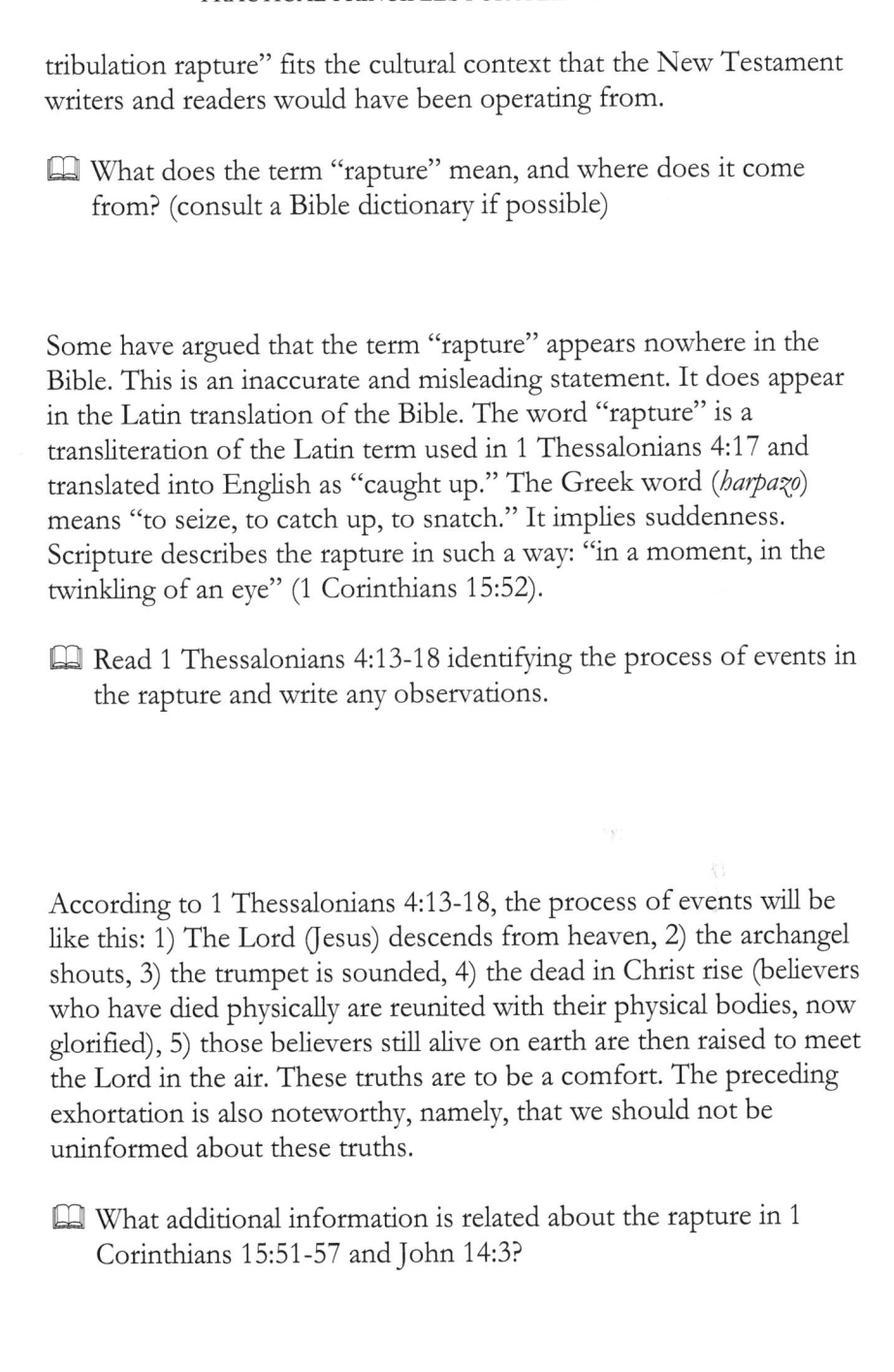

📖 What does the term "rapture" mean, and where does it come from? (consult a Bible dictionary if possible)

Some have argued that the term "rapture" appears nowhere in the Bible. This is an inaccurate and misleading statement. It does appear in the Latin translation of the Bible. The word "rapture" is a transliteration of the Latin term used in 1 Thessalonians 4:17 and translated into English as "caught up." The Greek word (*harpazo*) means "to seize, to catch up, to snatch." It implies suddenness. Scripture describes the rapture in such a way: "in a moment, in the twinkling of an eye" (1 Corinthians 15:52).

📖 Read 1 Thessalonians 4:13-18 identifying the process of events in the rapture and write any observations.

According to 1 Thessalonians 4:13-18, the process of events will be like this: 1) The Lord (Jesus) descends from heaven, 2) the archangel shouts, 3) the trumpet is sounded, 4) the dead in Christ rise (believers who have died physically are reunited with their physical bodies, now glorified), 5) those believers still alive on earth are then raised to meet the Lord in the air. These truths are to be a comfort. The preceding exhortation is also noteworthy, namely, that we should not be uninformed about these truths.

📖 What additional information is related about the rapture in 1 Corinthians 15:51-57 and John 14:3?

First Corinthians 15:51-57 teaches that we will not all "sleep" (die – in other words, some will be alive when the Lord comes back, and thus never have to taste death), but we shall all be changed (glorified, made imperishable and immortal – verse 53). John 14:3 makes it clear that Jesus will definitely come for believers and escort them to where He is.

📖 What is the difference between the rapture and the 2nd coming?

Regardless of when you believe the rapture will take place (Pre, mid, or post-tribulation), it has to be viewed as separate from the second coming. The rapture is when we meet Christ in the air (1 Thessalonians 4:13-18), the second coming is when Christ sets foot on earth (Revelation 19:11-21; Zechariah 14:4). Even if you believe these events will both occur at the end of the tribulation, they must be viewed as separate and distinct events.

The Seven Days

📖 What is the cultural picture of the bridegroom and the bride in the seven day period between the groom coming for the bride and his presentation of her?

Culturally, in a Jewish wedding, the seven days between the groom coming to get the bride and his presentation of her, involved the feasting and celebration of the wedding ceremony. According to Revelation 19, the marriage of the Lamb and the marriage supper are what will occupy the saints during the tribulation. Note that the marriage and marriage supper occur before the second coming according to Revelation 19.

📖 What according to Daniel 9:26-27 and 2 Thessalonians 2 will these days hold for the rest of the earth?

Daniel 9 teaches us much about these events we are studying. We see first that seventy weeks (lit. "periods of seven") are prophesied. We know that these are not literal weeks of days, for this would not fit history. But if they are viewed as periods of seven years, it fits neatly with history. Daniel divides these weeks into three segments. The first segment (7 weeks or 49 years – verse 25) is how long it took Nehemiah to rebuild the walls and moat around Jerusalem after the decree by Cyrus to rebuild. From this point to the crucifixion of Christ is 62 weeks (434 years, which when added to the 49 years fits the time frame from Cyrus' decree until Christ). Then Messiah is "cut off and has nothing" and the people of the prince who is to come will destroy Jerusalem and the temple (the prince is anti-Christ and his people are the Romans who in fact destroyed the city and sanctuary in 70 A.D.). There is a parenthesis at this point and the church age or age of grace transpires. Though the sixty-nine weeks have already been fulfilled, we are still waiting for the seventieth week. This prince who is to come (anti-Christ) will make a peace covenant with the many (Israel) for one week (the seventieth week - seven years) but breaks it half-way through and shuts down the temple service (apparently the temple has been rebuilt and priestly functions re-established) and the last half of the tribulation brings desolation and destruction. 2 Thessalonians 2 teaches us that these days will bring lawlessness (verse 7), satanic activity (verse 9), deception (verse 10), delusion (verse 11), and wickedness (verse 12). Revelation chapters 6-19 detail the horrors of this period much more graphically.

The Presentation Of The Bride

📖 What according to Zechariah 14:1-4 and Revelation 19:11-21 will the 2nd coming be like, and where and when will it occur?

Zechariah teaches us that these days will hold: a) a gathering of all the nations to war against Jerusalem - Armageddon (verse 2), b) a destruction and persecution of Jerusalem (verse 2), c) the Lord's intervention (verse 3), and d) the Lord's setting foot on earth on the Mount of Olives in Jerusalem (verse 4). This will bring to an end the seventieth week or the tribulation period. When Christ sets foot on the Mount of Olives it will split from east to west. It is interesting that geologists have identified a fault line running east to west on the Mount of Olives. Revelation 19 describes in detail the conquering work of Christ at Armageddon. We will go with Christ when He returns to earth, for we have the promise of 1 Thessalonians 4:17 that from the point of the rapture onward we will always be with the Lord Jesus.

The Application

📖 Read 1 John 3:3 and identify the application to the believer of the Lord's return.

Christians often made the mistake of deducing that although prophecy and eschatology are interesting, they are of little relevance or practical value to our lives today. That is not the case. Living in light of the Lord's eminent return ought to affect the way we live today. One specific application we find here in 1 John is that the one whose hope is the appearing of Christ purifies himself. The eminent return of the Lord ought to motivate us toward holiness.

📖 Read Matthew 24:42 and 1 Thessalonians 5:4 and identify the application to the believer of the Lord's return.

The primary application of these passages is preparedness, maintaining a readiness of heart and life so that there is no cause for shame or disappointment at Christ's return.

📖 Read Hebrews 10:24-25 and 1 Thessalonians 4:18 and identify the application to the believer of the Lord's return.

In these verses we find another application, namely, encouragement. Hebrews indicates that the closer we get to our Lord's coming, the more we need to be encouraging each other. In Hebrews 3:13 we see the flip side of this truth: if we do not encourage one another, there is the danger of becoming hardened by the "deceitfulness of sin." One of the ways we can encourage one another, according to 1 Thessalonians 4:18, is to comfort one another with the truths of prophecy.

📖 Read Matthew 24:14 and 28:18-20 and identify the application to the believer of the Lord's return.

In Matthew 24:14 we see that the job to be done before the Lord's return is the preaching of the gospel to the whole world. In Matthew 28:18-20 we see that we are to occupy ourselves with the task of making disciples, of baptizing, and of teaching obedience until "the end of the age." Ministry is a temporary opportunity, and as such, should not be neglected.

📖 Read 1 Thessalonians 4:13 and identify the application to the believer of the Lord's return.

A final application is to maintain at eternal perspective, especially as it relates to the death of loved ones. From the vantage point of eternity, death is nothing to be feared, but rather is to be welcomed by the child of God. Without this eternal perspective, we might be tempted toward the hopeless grief of the unbeliever.

*NOTE: After the application project for this lesson in your workbook are two appendices that will give you valuable information on this subject. Appendix B is a detailed explanation of why I personally do not believe the church will go through the tribulation.

Application Project ➡️

"But I am afraid, lest as the serpent deceived Eve by his craftiness, your minds should be led astray by the simplicity and purity of devotion to Christ." - 2 Corinthians 11:3

One of the most exciting aspects of the Christian faith is the future. We have much to look forward to, and if we keep this glorious future in focus it will radically affect our walk with God. The apostle Paul admonished the believers in Thessalonica, "we do not want you to be uninformed brethren about those who have fallen asleep (died) that you may not grieve as those who have no hope." And then he went on to detail our Christian hope, and stated, "comfort one another with these words." Since we are to not be uniformed" and these words are to be a "comfort", it is important that each believer see what the Scriptures say about the rapture and second coming. In 2 Timothy 4 there is an interesting contrast. In verse 8 Paul refers to all those "who have loved His appearing." In verse 10 he refers to Demas as "having loved this present world." It seems our hearts go one way or the other. Consider the following as you cultivate a love for His appearing.

1. What ministers to you most as you consider the truths about the second coming?

2. What things get in the way of your "love for His appearing?

3. How well informed are you of what the Scriptures teach about our Christian hope?

4. Second Timothy 3:16 states "all Scripture is inspired by God and is profitable for TEACHING, for REPROOF, for CORRECTION, and for TRAINING IN RIGHTEOUSNESS." With that as an outline, consider the following for application:

A. TEACHING: What from this passage do I need to believe?

B. REPROOF: Is there any sin I need to confess?

C. CORRECTION: What do I need to do differently?

D. TRAINING IN RIGHTEOUSNESS: What is my main application point? (make it specific and measurable)

Who is going to hold me accountable to this?

When am I going to do it? (put it in your schedule)

The most important thing in the Christian life is not what you know, but what you do with what you know (James 1:22, Luke 6:46).

Reminder:

John 14:15 states "if you love Me you will keep My commandments" and then in verses 16-17 Christ explains how we do that – ("and I will ask the Father, and He will give you another Helper...that is the Spirit..."). It is all-important that as we look at the applications God calls us to in His word, we recognize that we will only be able to accomplish those as we draw on the power of His Spirit indwelling us. Otherwise we will find ourselves trying to obey God through self-effort and we will ultimately fail. We see this necessity even in Christ. As John 14:10 puts it, "...the Father abiding in Me does His works." Why not take a moment to pray about this and give it to the Lord.

Appendix A - Definition of Terms

Eschatology: Greek word (from *"eschatos"*, extreme last, and *"logos"*, study) meaning the study of last things.

Rapture: Transliterated Latin word meaning to be "caught up" – the coming of Christ in the air for His saints in order that they might be with Him (1 Thessalonians 4:13-18; 1 Corinthians 15:51-57; John 14:1-3).

Tribulation: Seven years prior to Second Coming (Jeremiah 30:7-10; Daniel 9:24-27)

Second Coming: coming of Christ to the earth with His saints. (Revelation 19:11-21; Zechariah 14:4)

Millennium: The one thousand year reign of Christ on earth, fulfilling the Abrahamic and Davidic covenants. (Revelation 20:1-15)

Pre-Millennial View: The second coming is before the millennium. ORDER: 1) Church age ends at tribulation, 2) Second coming, 3) Millennium, 4) Judgment and eternity. This view expects a literal fulfillment of Scriptural promises to Israel.

Post-Millennial View: The second coming occurs after the millennium. ORDER: 1) Last one thousand years of the church age is the millennium (peace and abundance by church's efforts fulfills Revelation 20), 2) Second coming, 3) General resurrection, 4) Judgment and eternity, This view spiritualizes the promises to Israel as fulfilled in the church.

Amillennial View: The second coming is at end of church age with no earthly millennium (strictly, this view sees the present state of righteous in heaven is millennium). ORDER: 1) Second coming, 2) General resurrection, 3) Judgment and eternity. This view spiritualizes promises to Israel as fulfilled in the church.

Pre-Tribulation Rapture: The rapture occurs sometime before the tribulation (Revelation 3:10, 6:17; 2 Thessalonians 2; 1 Thessalonians 1:10,5:6,9; Revelation 4:1 – a picture of rapture).

Mid-Tribulation Rapture: The rapture occurs half-way through tribulation. This view sees the tribulation as only the last half of the seven years when God's wrath is manifest. (1 Corinthians 15:52; Revelation 11:15,16; 12:16; Revelation 11 is a picture of the rapture).

Post-Tribulation Rapture: Rapture occurs at the end of tribulation (rapture and tribulation are described the same, God's people are protected from wrath [e.g. plagues of Egypt] while going through it, the saints are on earth during the tribulation – Matthew 24:22).

Appendix B—The Church and the Tribulation

I. The Purpose of the Tribulation
   A. It is a time for Israel
      1. Daniel 9:24,27 "for your city and your people"
      2. Deuteronomy 4:29-30 "when you are in distress in the last days"
      3. Jeremiah 30:7-10 "the time of Jacob's (Israel's) distress"
      4. Revelation 7:4-8 "sealed from every tribe of the sons of Israel"
   B. It is a time for God's wrath
      1. Revelation 6:16-17 "the great day of their wrath has come"
      2. Revelation 14:10,19 "the wine of the wrath of God"
      3. Zephaniah 1:18 "the day of the Lord's wrath"
   C. It is a time of Satanic Authority
      1. Revelation 9:1-11 "out of the bottomless pit...came forth locusts" (Jude 6; 2 Peter 2:4; Luke 8:31)
      2. Revelation 13:1-9 "who is like the beast?"

II. The Promises to the Church
   A. 1 Thessalonians 5:9 "for God has not destined us for wrath"
   B. 1 Thessalonians 1:10 "Jesus who delivers us from the wrath to come"
   C. 2 Thessalonians 2:13 "God has chosen us from the beginning for salvation" (salvation from what? context implies tribulation)
   D. Revelation 3:10 "I will keep you from the hour of testing"
   E. 2 Peter 2:9 "The Lord knows how to rescue the godly" (God consistently delivers the righteous before He judges the unrighteous)
   F. Matthew 16:18 "the gates of Hades (Hell) shall not overpower it" (compare this with Revelation 13:7)

III. The Presentation of the Rapture
   A. Matthew 24:44 "the Son of man is coming when you do not think He will)
   B. Matthew 24:36 "of that day and hour no one knows"

C. James 5:8 "the coming of the Lord is at hand" (if the rapture is to occur at an unknown time it cannot be at the middle or end of the tribulation since we would be able to calculate that from the signing of the "peace covenant" with the Anti-Christ and Israel)
  D. Titus 2:13 "looking for the blessed hope" (if the rapture is not first we should look for the Anti-Christ first, not Christ – Romans 8:24-25)

IV. The Population of the Millennium
  A. THE PREDICTION: There will be mortal bodies in the Millennial kingdom (Isaiah 11:6-8; Revelation 20:7-9)

  B. THE PROBLEM: If at the end of the Tribulation all believers are raptured and all unbelievers are destroyed there would be no mortal bodies left to populate the millennium (requires a Pre-tribulation rapture).

LESSON THREE

"RADICAL CHRISTIANS LIVE BY A RADICAL POWER"

John 14:8-31

The Picture Of Indwelling Power (14:8-14)

 What is the significance of Philip's response and how Christ answers it?

It is obvious from Philip's response that he did not understand what Christ was trying to say in verse 7: "If you had known me, you would have known My Father also; from now on you know Him, and have seen Him." Jesus' point is, "if you really understood who I was, you'd know that to see Me is to see the Father." The Greek word for "known" means "to know by experience" and is in the "Pluperfect tense" which refers to completed action in the past tense. It must have been confusing for the disciples to hear Jesus suggest that they had not known Him after they had spent three years with Him. Philip sidesteps that issue and says, "Show us the Father and we'll be satisfied." Christ's answer brings things back to focus. He is saying, "Have I been with you so long and you still haven't come to recognize who I really am?" The statement, "He who has seen Me has seen the Father," is one of Christ's clearest assertions to deity.

📖 What does the phrase "the Father abiding in Me does His works" mean, and how do the beliefs mentioned at the first of the verse relate?

The phrase "the Father abiding in Me does His works" communicates a powerful message to the believer. If Christ, as the man/God, did not do the works of ministry on His own, but was dependent on God the Father doing them through Him, how much more is it necessary for our ministry to flow from surrender and not self-effort. If our ministry is not God working through us, but mere human striving, it will amount to nothing. The beliefs mentioned at the first of the verse relate back to Philip's statement.

📖 What according to verse 11 are the two reasons to believe in Christ (note the contrasting word, "otherwise")?

Basically, Jesus is saying, "You can believe Me because I say it, or you can believe Me because you see it." Everything Jesus did was consistent with what He said.

📖 What are the parameters of the promised potential to believers in verse 12?

How does Christ going to the Father relate to this, and should this be taken literally?

This is perhaps one of the most radical statements in the New Testament. Christ prefaces it by saying "Truly, truly" (literally, "amen, amen" – "it is true, it is true") so that there will be no doubt that He really means what He says. Jesus is saying that the one who believes has the potential of both equaling and exceeding the works of Jesus. There is no indication of any limit to this, and the promise is not made just to the disciples, but to "he who believes in Me." Christ going to the Father is significant because, as He will explain shortly, unless He does, the Holy Spirit will not come. The only reason we would not take this promise literally is because unfortunately, few live lives that are characterized by such power, but the truth is, the problem is on our end not His.

📖 How according to verses 13-14 will the "greater works" be accomplished, and what are the limits of this?

Verse 13 begins with "and" showing that it is not a separate thought but a continuation of the previous one These two verses show us how to experience these greater works. God intends that the greater works be accomplished in response to believing prayer. Notice that in verse 12 Jesus says the believer will do greater works; in verse 13 He clarifies that in actuality it is He who does the works ("I will do it"). Probably the disciples' eyes bugged out at this point so Jesus repeats Himself in verse 14 to make sure they get the message. There are no limits to this promise; Jesus says, "Whatever you ask...", and "If you ask Me anything...".

📖 What does it mean to "ask in My [Christ's] name" and what is to be our motive for doing so?

"In Jesus' name" is more than a spiritual way of saying "the end." To pray in Jesus' name involves acknowledging that we enter the presence of God because of the work of Christ on the cross (Hebrews 10:19). It is an acknowledgment that the Father hears me because Jesus is righteous, not because I am. Our motive for coming to the Father and asking Him to do the things that only He can do is "that the Father may be glorified in the Son."

The Purpose Of Indwelling Power (14:15-24)

📖 What does verse 15 reveal as the motive for our obedience?

Verse 15 shows us that the motive for obedience is love, not wrath. Obedience that flows from wrath is hypocrisy. If it takes the fear of punishment to motivate us, then our actions do not flow from our character. Our obedience is not of the heart. The Pharisees were diligent in pursuing obedience, but their motive was self-oriented, not others-focused; it was pride, not love of God.

📖 Why does verse 16 begin with the word "and," and what is the significance of this?

There is a real danger here of putting the cart before the horse. While it is true that if we love the Lord, we will have a heart to obey, this truth taken by itself leads to slavery. The word "and" makes it clear that the way we obey is the ministry of the Holy Spirit in our lives. We cannot obey without God's help, the "Helper." Not understanding this, many struggle with trying to muster enough striving and self-effort to prove that they really do love Jesus, and with feelings of doubt when they fail to do so. But failure is inevitable without the empowering work of the Spirit. If Jesus could not do the works of the Father on His own but was dependent on the Father doing His works through Him (verse 10), how much more needy are we?

📖 What does the Greek word translated "another" in verse 16 mean, and how according to verse 17 will He "be with you forever"?

There are two Greek words for "another": *heteros*, which means another that is qualitatively different, and *allos*, which means another that is the same (this is where our English word "ally" comes from). It is the later that is used here, and the point is, the Holy Spirit is just as much God as Jesus is. Verse 17 shows us that the way the Holy Spirit is with us forever is by coming to indwell us. The Holy Spirit is God, resident in the human heart.

📖 What does the title, "Spirit of truth" mean and what is the significance of the switch from "He" (verse 17) to "I" (verse 18)?

The title, "spirit of truth" indicates that truth is an integral part of His nature. The word "truth" appears in the Greek with the definite article. This is significant in this sense: without the definite article it would mean "truth in general, any truth." With the definite article it would mean "specific truth." It could be translated "the Spirit of THE truth" for it points not to truth as an idea but to ultimate truth which is part of who God is. In verse 18 Jesus switches in mid thought from speaking of the Holy Spirit coming to saying "I will come to you." It would seem from the context that He is trying to say that He and the Holy Spirit are one.

📖 What day is verse 18-20 referring to and when will this occur?

At a casual glance it might appear that this is referring to the second coming, but this cannot be so. The word translated "a little while" here is *mikron* (from which the prefix "micro" is derived) and means a very short measure. It is the same word used in 13:33 when Jesus says, "I am with you a little while longer." There He is speaking of His eminent death and departure, and there is good reason to think He has the same thing in view here. Notice that He says, "the world will behold Me no more; but you will behold Me." This cannot be the second coming, for then even unbelievers will see Him. It makes more sense that He is speaking of the advent of the Holy Spirit, for we do not have to wait until the 2nd coming to know that Jesus is in the Father and we are in Him and He is in us.

📖 What do verses 21, 23 and 24 reveal about the measure of our love for Christ, and what will result from our obedience (or lack of it)?

The important thing to notice there is that obedience is a result of, not a reason for, our relationship with God. If we want to see more obedience in our lives, we need to develop our love relationship with God. Obedience that does not flow from a relationship with God is man-centered righteousness and man's righteousness is filthy rags to the Lord.

📖 Identify the logic of the question in verse 22 and how Christ answers it.

It makes sense that someone would ask why Jesus is not going to disclose Himself to the world. After all, isn't the reason He came, to disclose Himself and the Father to the world? Jesus doesn't really answer the question here. It is not until 15:27 that He begins indicating that the way in which Jesus will reveal Himself to the world is through His followers. He will develop this idea more fully in 17:13-21 where He relates that the result of the Father being in Him and Him being in the disciples will be that the world will believe in Him. This is "incarnational evangelism" – Christ in us in the world. Christ's answer to the question in essence is, "I will disclose Myself to you, and you will disclose Me to the world."

📖 Compare verse 23 with Ephesians 3:14-17 and identify the meaning of the phrase, "make our abode with him."

In Ephesians 3:17 Paul prays for the Ephesian believers that Christ might dwell in their hearts. But an important truth is that he is writing to people who are already believers. This isn't speaking simply of Christ indwelling someone, but rather, it would seem, of Him being completely at home in their lives. It would seem perhaps that Jesus is communicating this same idea here. The one walking in fellowship and obedience with Christ is a fit dwelling place for the King of Kings and Lord of Lords.

The Prospect Of Indwelling Power (25,26)

📖 What does the Greek word "helper" mean as it is applied to the Holy Spirit?

The Greek word translated "Helper" here, *parakletos*, is derived from *para*, to the side of, and *kaleo*, to call. It has the idea of one called alongside to help. It is the Spirit of God who comes along side us (actually, indwells us) to help us live the Christian life. We cannot live a life that pleases God in our own efforts. If we could, Christ's death on the cross is wasted. It is the ongoing ministry of the Holy Spirit to direct and empower us as we yield to Him.

📖 What according to verse 26 are the main ministries of the Holy Spirit in the life of the believer?

He teaches us truth and He reminds us of what Jesus teaches us. The truth of God cannot be understood simply by reasoning, it requires revelation. If it took the illumining work of God's Spirit for men to write Scripture, then it will also take illumination to understand it. Heresy results from people trying to understand and interpret God's word without the revealing ministry of the Spirit. The second ministry is one of prompting and reminding. We are not limited to

Scripture we can remember through cramming. The Spirit is able to bring to mind a verse long forgotten whenever we are in need.

The Peace Of Indwelling Power (14:27-31)

📖 What is the significance of the command, "let not your heart be troubled, nor let it be fearful" and how do we do that?

It is especially significant that in the Greek it is an imperative, meaning a command, not a suggestion. God would not command it if we were not able, by the Sprit's empowering, to fulfill it. This indicates that not being fearful or anxious is a choice. This does not mean that to have emotions of fear or anxiety are sin. It is sin however to let those emotions control us. It is significant that the admonition is in the context of the ministry of the Holy Spirit in our lives. Galatians 5:22 indicates that peace is part of the "fruit of the Spirit." We appropriate this as we yield our lives to Him and as we keep our eyes on the Lord instead of our circumstances.

📖 What does Christ mean by the statement, "if you loved (*agape*) Me..." and in what way is the Father greater than Christ if Christ and the Father are one?

The word "loved" is in the imperfect tense, which is a little difficult to translate into English. It refers to continuous or linear action in past time. It is not simply, completed action, but ongoing action. In other words, He isn't saying, "You don't love Me," but rather, "You haven't consistently loved Me unconditionally." *Agape* means love that is not circumstantial or conditional. As to the idea that the

Father is greater, this does not detract from Christ's deity, but rather, points out the limitations He took on when He entered time and space in human form.

📖 Why according to verse 29 was Christ telling the disciples all that was coming, and how does that apply to us?

Christ was telling them in advance what was to happen for two reasons. First, He wanted to prepare the disciples for the rough road ahead. Second, and primarily according to the text, it attested to His deity to foretell the future, and helped them to believe. For us today, the prophesies of Scripture should be viewed in the same light.

📖 What exactly is verse 30 saying?

"I will not speak much more with you," seems to be an indication of the shortness of time. "For the ruler of this world (Satan) is coming," points not to Satan coming to the world, but to his coming at Christ in the crucifixion plot. "He has nothing in Me," is a reflection of the truth that though Satan is the "ruler of this world," he is not the ruler of Christ, and cannot in Him find any propensity to sin or grounds for condemnation.

📖 What specifically is Christ referring to in verse 31, and where was He going?

In verse 31 we see demonstrated in Christ the very truth He just preached to the disciples, namely that obedience is an indication of a love relationship with the Father. Christ was demonstrating His love for the Father by obediently following the course to the cross. When He says, "let us go from here," He knows He is heading to the cross.

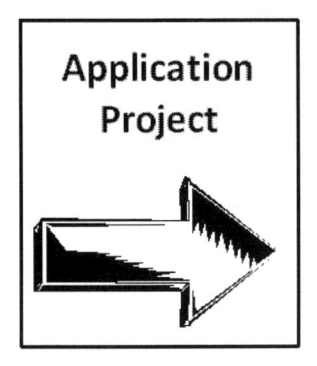

Application Project

"But I am afraid, lest as the serpent deceived Eve by his craftiness, your minds should be led astray from the simplicity and purity of devotion to Christ"
- 2 Corinthians 11:3

The Christian life, that is, as God intends it to be, is a life of purpose and power. In Ephesians chapter one, Paul prayed that the "eyes of our heart" would grasp the power of God that is ours because we are His. We experience this power for living when we are "filled" (directed and empowered) by the Spirit of God. The problem is that our lives, much like a car, have only one driver's seat. If we insist on directing our own lives then God steps aside, but fortunately He never leaves us (Hebrews 13:5). He is still "resident" in our lives but no longer "president." The result is a powerless walk that bears no fruit. In the same way that salvation is God's work, not man's, the Christian life is God's responsibility. To experience it as God intends we must "be filled with the Spirit" (Ephesians 5:18). Consider the following as you pursue a more radical Christianity.

1. What successes have you seen in your Christian life as a result of being "Spirit-filled"?

2. In what areas of your relationship with God do you most need a sense of power?

3. What things tend to get in the way of you seeing God's power at work?

4. Second Timothy 3:16 states "all Scripture is inspired by God and is profitable for TEACHING, for REPROOF, for CORRECTION, and for TRAINING IN RIGHTEOUSNESS." With that as an outline, consider the following for application:
A. TEACHING: What from this passage do I need to believe?

B. REPROOF: Is there any sin I need to confess?

C. CORRECTION: What do I need to do differently?

D. TRAINING IN RIGHTEOUSNESS: What is my main application point? (make it specific and measurable)

Who is going to hold me accountable to this?

When am I going to do it? (put it in your schedule)

The most important thing in the Christian life is not what you know, but what you do with what you know (James 1:22, Luke 6:46).

Reminder:
John 14:15 states "if you love Me you will keep My commandments" and then in verses 16-17 Christ explains how we do that - ("and I will ask the Father, and He will give you another Helper...that is the Spirit..."). It is all-important that as we look at the applications God calls us to in His word, we recognize that we will only be able to accomplish those as we draw on the power of His Spirit indwelling us. Otherwise we will find ourselves trying to obey God through self-effort and we will ultimately fail. We see this necessity even in Christ. As John 14:10 puts it, "...the Father abiding in Me does His works." Why not take a moment to pray about this and give it to the Lord.

LESSON FOUR

"RADICAL CHRISTIANS HAVE A RADICAL PURPOSE"

John 15:1-17

The Preparation Of The Believer (15:1-3)

📖 Identify the analogy Christ uses here and who fills each role, and write any observations.

In Christ's analogy there are three roles: a) the grapevine which represents Christ, b) the gardener who is a picture of the Father, and c) the branches, representative of believers. It is noteworthy that in a number of Old Testament passages (e.g. Psalm 80:8-19; Isaiah 5:1; Jeremiah 2:21; Exodus 19:10; Hosea 10:1) the vine is used as an ancient symbol of God's people.

📖 What does it mean in verse 2 for a branch to be "taken away" and how does this apply to the believer?

The Greek word translated "takes away" (*airo*) literally means "to lift." There are two ways you can interpret this verse. One view is that Jesus is saying a fruitless branch is removed, in which case it probably refers to the idea that God might take a fruitless Christian home early rather than allow His name to be maligned. *Airo* is translated "remove" in John 11:30. Another view is that the word shouldn't be taken to mean "lift away" here but rather, "lift up", in which case the point would be that a fruitless branch is propped up to make it easier for it to bear fruit. *Airo* is translated "picked up" in John 8:59. What this verse is not teaching is that Christians who do not bear fruit lose their salvation.

📖 What does it mean in verse 2 for a branch to be "pruned" and how does this apply to the believer?

In vine dressing pruning involves cutting away superfluous growth in order that the energy of the plant is spent bearing fruit instead of growing more leaves. The primary tool of God to "prune" the lives of believers of things that aren't fruitful and to shape their character to make them more fruitful is His word.

📖 What does it mean to be "clean" and how does the Word do this?

The word "clean" here is the same root word as "prune" in verse 2. God's Word when rightly responded to cleanses, purifies and purges our life.

The Process For The Believer (15:4-6)

📖 Here in verse 4 Christ continues the analogy of the vine and the branches. How do the truths about bearing fruit relate to the believer?

Christ's point is that to bear fruit, a believer must stay connected to Him just as a branch must stay connected to the vine. When you examine a grape vine, the branches with the strongest connection to the vine are the ones with the most grapes.

📖 What does the word "abide" mean, and how do we do that?

The call to "abide" is a Greek imperative, a command and not a suggestion. As to exactly what it means to "abide in Christ," John answers this in 1 John 3:24 – "…and the one who keeps His commandments abides in Him, and He in him." We "abide" in Christ so long as we walk in obedient fellowship with Him. When there is unconfessed sin that we refuse to deal with, we are no longer abiding. We see the same truth here in John 15:10. It is our fellowship with Christ which produces the fruit of ministry, not the striving of human effort.

📖 Experientially we know that there are things we can do apart from Christ. How should we take this statement that apart from Him we can do "nothing"?

It is true that a Christian can witness, lead Bible studies, coordinate Christian activities, be involved in protests, etc. even if they are not abiding in fellowship with the Lord. But these are not fruit. They are only activities we associate with fruit, on a par with grape-picking. But grape-picking is a futile activity when there are no ripe grapes to pick. From the vantage point of eternity, all Christians effort that does not flow from an abiding life is meaningless and amounts to nothing. In the Greek there are two words for negatives: *me*, which means a negative possibility, and *ou*, which means an absolute negative. It is the latter which is used here.

📖 Identify the ramifications of the warning in verse 6 and exactly what they mean to the believer.

The phrase "thrown away" here is translated from a different word that "takes away" in verse 2. This word means "to cast, or throw." The believer who does not abide in Christ is "cast aside" (not used). They are put on a shelf by the Lord, for they are unusable to Him. The second point Jesus makes is that they "dry up." There is no relationship with God without abiding fellowship. The final pronouncement is that such branches are "cast into the fire and ... burned." While some view this as a reference to hell, this would be inconsistent with the clear teaching of Scripture elsewhere. It is more likely that this points to the fact that at the judgment seat of Christ, the works of the flesh (wood, hay, and straw) are burned up. This burning does not impact salvation but rather, reward (see 1 Corinthians 3:10-15).

The Product Of The Believer (15:7-15)

📖 What according to verse 7 are the criteria for answered prayer and what does it mean for Christ's words to "abide" in us?

The criteria for answered prayer here are a) that we abide in Him, b) that His words abide in us, and c) that we ask what we wish. While some may think this an impossibility, there is no real way to take the verse other than literally. The qualifier however, hinges on the two prerequisites of abiding in Him and His words abiding in us. As we do this, our very wishes become aligned with His. Psalm 37:4 says, "Delight yourself in the Lord; and He will give you the desires of your heart." The point here is the same: when our delight is in the Lord, our desires align themselves with His will.

📖 What exactly is it that glorifies the Father, the truth that precedes it or what follows?

At first glance it appears that what glorifies the Father is us bearing much fruit and proving to be His disciples. But the Greek word translated "that" in verse 8 can be translated, "to the end that" or "in order that." It seems to make more sense to view it this way. The result is that the phrase, "By this is My Father glorified" becomes linked with the preceding verse. In other words, the Father is glorified by us abiding and asking, and the result of this is bearing fruit and proving to be His disciples

📖 What exactly is Christian fruit, and how does much of it prove us to be Christ's disciples?

While we tend to associate the idea of fruit with ministry, the Scriptural use of the term most often points to the fruit of Christian character. The most familiar such use is Galatians 5:22-23 where nine character qualities are listed as the "fruit of the Spirit." Some other

PRACTICAL PRINCIPLES FOR A LIFE OF POWER

related passages are : Ephesians 5:9 ("the fruit of light, which consists in all goodness, righteousness and truth"), Philippians 1:11 ("the fruit of righteousness"), and James 3:18 ("the seed whose fruit is righteousness"). The idea of ministry being fruit also appears, but less frequently. Some examples are: Romans 1:13 (Paul speaks of "obtaining some fruit among them"), Romans 15:28 (giving is called "fruit"), and Colossians 1:10 ("bearing fruit in every good word"). As to how much fruit proves us to be His disciples, in Matthew 12:33 Jesus says, "the tree is known by its fruit." It is in fruit-bearing that the identity of the tree is most clearly seen. Ryrie points out a progression here: the step from fruit to more fruit involves pruning (cleansing) through the Word of God (verse 2), and the step from more fruit to much fruit involves a life of answered prayer (verse 7).

📖 How does the love of God mentioned in verse 9 relate here, and what according to verse 10 is our response?

God's love is what keeps us walking with Him. In fact, our love for Him is always in response to His love for us. 1 John 4:19 says we love because He first loved us. Here in verse 10 we see the primary way we express our love for God: obedience. Note that this does not teach obedience as the reason for God's love for us, but rather, the result of us understanding and experiencing His love for us. It is our obedience however, that enables us to "abide in His love." When we are disobedient, it must be dealt with by confession and repentance, or else we will cease to experience God's love.

📖 What according to verse 11 is the result of abiding in Christ's love and obeying His commands?

According to verse 11, a lifestyle of experiencing God's love and walking in obedience results in joy. If there is no joy in our Christian life, we have lost sight of God's love and forgiveness, and we are no longer abiding in Him.

📖 What is the significance of us being commanded to love as Christ loves and how does He love?

The word for "love" here is *agape*, and means committed, unconditional love. Notice that in John 13:34 Jesus calls this a "new commandment." Here, on the same evening He repeats this new commandment, and again in verse 17. It seems to be a point of some importance. In John 13:35 Jesus told them, "By this all men will know that you are My disciples, if you have love for one another." In light of what we just looked at in question 3, the idea of loving one another is obviously high on Jesus' list of what constitutes fruit. The measure of our love for each other is to be Christ's love for us. Fulfilling such a call is impossible apart from abiding in Him and experiencing His love for us.

📖 How does the statement of verse 13 relate with verse 12?

Obviously the main point to this statement is the fact that Christ was going to the cross. Romans 5:8 says that "God demonstrates His own love toward us in that while we were yet sinners, Christ died for us." There is a second truth here though that must be seen. While dying physically is a great expression of love, in our day-to-day relationships we have little opportunity for such expression. We can, however, die to our own selfish desires. We can die to our longing to put self first in everything, and in so doing we put others first. This is an act of faith, for when we so live, we are trusting God and not self to meet the needs of self.

📖 What do verses 13-15 reveal about our relationship with Christ and what does it mention as a result of that?"

In these verses we see that the Christian life is not slavery to God but friendship with Him. What a powerful concept! The Creator of the universe invites me to abide with Him in friendship. This is very much a New Testament concept. Abraham was called "the friend of God" but that was viewed as an exception by the Jews, not as the norm. The phrase "No longer" indicates a change in policy. They are no longer servants, as they were while under the law of the Old Covenant. The result of such a relationship.

The Purpose Of The Believer (15:16-17)

📖 What is the cultural significance of the disciples being chosen instead of choosing Him as their teacher?

In the rabbinical structure of the day, each rabbi (teacher) selected His own disciples. As such, it was understood that when selected by a rabbi, the honor came with great responsibility. It was the job of the disciple to do everything the rabbi ordered. This truth relates equally to all believers. Each of us was chosen of God before the foundation of the world (Ephesians 1:4).

📖 What according to verse 16 was Christ's purpose for choosing us?

We were chosen, not simply as the object of Christ's affection, but for the purpose of bearing fruit that would remain. The phrase "bear fruit" is in the present tense, meaning to continually bear fruit. As we saw earlier, the fruit of the Christian life is primarily character, though it also encompasses ministry.

📖 Why does Christ add that our fruit should remain, and how does prayer relate to this?

The word "remain" here is used in the absolute sense, with the idea of perpetuity. In other words, our fruit is to be eternal. If our fruit is the result of God's word in and through us, it will be. This is the idea Paul is communicating in 1 Corinthians 3:10-15 when he speaks of the judgment of the believers' works. The idea of answered prayer is linked here, because fruit that is a result of prayer is always fruit that God produces, not man.

📖 Why does Christ repeat Himself in verse 17?

The statement "this I command you, that you love one another" could equally be translated "All that I have commanded you tonight is to the end that you would love one another." The King James Translation ` "these things" is probably more clear than "this" as in the NAS. Christ is repeating Himself here because He is summarizing and emphasizing.

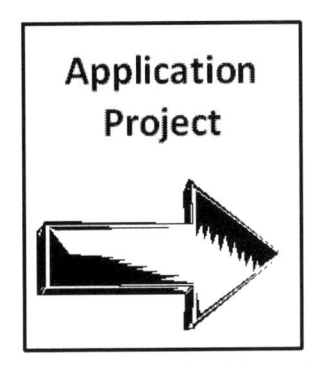

Application Project

"But I am afraid, lest as the serpent deceived Eve by his craftiness, your minds should be led astray from the simplicity and purity of devotion to Christ."
- 2 Corinthians 11:3

Christianity is not a religion, it is a personal relationship with the living God. Anything else falls short of what God desires. We see in Christ's letter of warning to the church at Ephesus (Revelation 2:1-7) that working for God is never to take the place of "simple, pure devotion" to Him (2 Corinthians 11:3). The greatest commandment, says Christ, is to "love the Lord your God with all your heart, soul, mind, and strength." Everything else hangs on doing that. One of the secrets of radical Christianity is learning to "abide" in Christ and to allow Him to bear fruit through us. This is what He desire to do. Consider the following as you pursue a more radical Christianity.

1. What things have aided in you developing intimacy with Christ?

2. What things tend to distract you from an abiding relationship with Christ?

3. Can you think of any examples in your life with the results of not abiding in Christ?

4. How well do you think you understand God's love for you, and how does that affect your relationship with Him?

5. Second Timothy 3:16 states "all Scripture is inspired by God and is profitable for TEACHING, for REPROOF, for CORRECTION, and for TRAINING IN RIGHTEOUSNESS." With that as an outline, consider the following for application:

A. TEACHING: What from this passage do I need to believe?

B. REPROOF: Is there any sin I need to confess?

C. CORRECTION: What do I need to do differently?

D. TRAINING IN RIGHTEOUSNESS: What is my main application point? (make it specific and measurable)

Who is going to hold me accountable to this?

When am I going to do it? (put it in your schedule)

The most important thing in the Christian life is not what you know, but what you do with what you know (James 1:22, Luke 6:46).

Reminder:

John 14:15 states "if you love Me you will keep My commandments" and then in verses 16-17 Christ explains how we do that - ("and I will ask the Father, and He will give you another Helper...that is the Spirit..."). It is all-important that as we look at the applications God calls us to in His word, we recognize that we will only be able to accomplish those as we draw on the power of His Spirit indwelling us. Otherwise we will find ourselves trying to obey God through self-effort and we will ultimately fail. We see this necessity even in Christ. As John 14:10 puts it, "...the Father abiding in Me does His works." Why not take a moment to pray about this and give it to the Lord.

LESSON FIVE

"RADICAL CHRISTIANS HAVE A RADICAL POTENTIAL"

John 15:18-16:15

The Potential Of Persecution (15:18-16:6)

📖 What according to verse 18 do we need to remind ourselves of when we are hated by the world, and how will this help?

We need to remind ourselves that the world hated Jesus first. The Greek structure of the word "if" (indicative mood with the conditional particle) assumes the fact as existing ("If the world hates you, as it does"). The call to "know" is a "present imperative" in the Greek, meaning that we are commanded to continually remind ourselves of this truth. The word "hate" is in the perfect tense pointing to a permanent attitude.

📖 What do verses 19-20 relate about why the world hates us and how to respond to that?

Unlike verse 18, the word "if" here is constructed in the Greek so as to carry the meaning of "if" with a negative assumption ("if you were of the world, but you are not"). The world hates us because we are not of the world, we do not belong to it. The "world" (*kosmos*) refers not to the planet itself, or to the populous of it in general, but to the present world order aligned with the "god of this world" (Satan) and standing in opposition to Christ and His coming kingdom. In the present scheme of things we must recognize that there is a price to be paid for walking with God in a world that does not. We must respond to the hate of the world with the understanding that we are receiving some of the blows meant for Jesus. We must not be surprised by persecution. In fact, we should be surprised if we do not encounter it, for the Word promises that "all who desire to live godly in Christ Jesus will be persecuted" (2 Timothy 3:12).

📖 Why according to verses 21-22 does the world hate Christ?

These verses list several reasons that the world hates Christ. First, because of His name's sake (Lit. "on account of My name"). The name of Christ represented the faith, the attitude, the claims and the aim of the disciples. His name was their confession. Martin Luther said, "The name of Christ from your mouth will be to them nothing but poison and death." A second reason the world hates Christ is because they do not know the Father, the one who sent Christ. Third, they hate Christ because His message and ministry expose their sin. Sin is always sin, but without truth it is not always seen as such. Jesus, the light of the world, shines into the darkness, but men whose deeds are dark do not like the light. Since we are salt and light in the world, we too expose dark deeds. The term "excuse" at the end of verse 22 is translated "cloak" in the KJV. This is closer to the idea of the Greek word. It doesn't mean that their sin would be excused, but that it would be hidden.

📖 How is hating Christ hating the Father, and what does Christ's works have to do with their sin?

Since the Father sent Christ, He is an ambassador for the Father. Hating Christ is woven into hating His purpose for being here, the task the Father sent Him for. As to what Christ's works have to do with their sin, since He worked the works that only God could do, they had no excuse for not believing. Rejecting Him therefore isn't based on their inability to believe, but their unwillingness to accept the consequences on their lives that believing dictates.

📖 What is the significance of the quote in verse 25 and the truth it relates?

The quote in verse 25 originates in Psalm 35:19 and Psalm 69:4. Both are Psalms of David lamenting the unjust hatred directed toward him, and here we see Jesus applying them to Himself. The truth here is that hatred doesn't always have a just reason. In this section we have seen that a) the world hates Christ (verse 18), b) His followers are aliens in the world (verse 19), c) the world will persecute believers because they follow Christ (verse 20), d) the persecutors do not know God (verse 21), and e) Jesus' words (verse 22) and his works (verse 24) rebuke them.

📖 What doctrines does verse 26 relate about the Holy Spirit and how does He assist us in persecution?

Here we see that the Spirit is a) a "helper", b) sent from the Father (as was Christ – verse 21), c) truth, d) proceeding from the Father (it is interesting that the word "proceeding" is in the present tense - it is not that the Spirit came from the Father, or will come from the

Father, but that He is ever coming from the Father continuously as the light is ever coming from the sun), and e) He will "bear witness of Christ." It is noteworthy that the Holy Spirit is mentioned here as our "Helper" in the context of persecution. It is only by His empowering work in our hearts that we are able to endure persecution.

📖 What is the significance of the Holy Spirit "bearing witness" and of the disciples also doing this?

If one of the ministries of the Holy Spirit is to bear witness of Christ, then when we are directed and empowered by this same Spirit, we too will bear witness of Christ. Acts 1:8 states, "...you shall receive power when the Holy Spirit has come upon you; and you shall be My witnesses both in Jerusalem, and in all Judea and Samaria, and even to the remotest part of the earth." A key point to recognize is that bearing witness of Christ isn't something that we have to strive to do. It is the inevitable consequence of being Spirit-filled.

📖 Why according to verses 1 and 4 is Christ telling the disciples these things and how does this relate to us?

Remember the context of this passage. It is the night before the crucifixion. These are Christ's last words, distilled to the most important things. Christ gives them two reasons here for telling them what He does: a) to keep them from stumbling (or falling away), and b) so that when persecution comes they won't be surprised and caught off guard. This all relates to us, for we too will encounter persecution and we need to know that up front.

📖 Identify from verses 2-3 what our persecutions will be like and who will be doing it.

We see here that the disciples would be cast out of the synagogue (their former center of religious, cultural and social life) and that their persecution would even go to the extent of murder. The key thing to see here is that it is those who are religious and yet do not know God who are the ringleaders (they think they are pleasing God by doing it). From the crucifixion of Christ to the stoning of Stephen all the way to today, it is the religious who most vehemently oppose the church. Religion without relationship is a most dangerous thing.

📖 Compare verse 4 with 14:26 and identify how the disciples would remember and interpret Christ's words.

In John 14:26 we see that one of the ministries of the Spirit is bringing to mind what Christ taught as well as teaching us to understand what He said.

📖 Why were the disciples sad about His leaving and what was wrong with their perspective?

From a human perspective it is easy to understand why the disciples were sad at the prospect of Christ leaving. He had poured His life into theirs for three years. Beyond that, they were expecting that this was the time of the kingdom. They couldn't comprehend that His dying was part of God's plan. The problem with their perspective is that they weren't looking from the vantage point of eternity, and they didn't understand that Christ had to go for the Spirit to come. And the Spirit had to come if they were to fulfill their role in God's plan.

📖 How does Christ's leaving relate to the coming of the Holy Spirit and why was one necessary for the other?

There are no clear answers to this question other than to say that it is so because Scripture says that it is so. The Greek word for "not" used here of the Helper is the word which denotes the absolute negative (If I do not go away, the Helper absolutely will not come). We see in John 7:39 the same idea as here: "But this He spoke of the Spirit, whom those who believed in Him were to receive; for the Spirit was not yet given, because Jesus was not yet glorified." Obviously there is a link between the two, and perhaps, though mysterious, we can gain some of an understanding by recognizing that in chapter 14:17-18 Jesus equated the coming of the Spirit with Him coming to them. While on the earth as a human, Jesus had the limitations of time and space; He could not be everywhere at once. After His glorification He once again had full use of His divinity, and thus returned to omnipresence. By this glorification it became possible for Christ to indwell every human heart that would receive Him in the person of the Holy Spirit.

The Potential Of Power (16:8-15)

📖 What does the Greek word for "conviction" mean and how does it differ from conversion?

The word "conviction" means to convince (usually to convince of error). Notice that the whole world will be convinced of sin, righteousness and judgment. But to be convinced is not enough, for unless we act on that knowledge it will not benefit. Demons are convinced of God but that does not save them (James 2:19). Conversion is not merely an intellectual acknowledgment or an emotional response, but requires a surrender of the will.

📖 What exactly is the point of verse 9?

The greatest sin, and in fact, the root sin, is unbelief, an unwillingness to trust God and take Him at His word. The Spirit will reveal this truth. Remember that one day "every knee will bow and every tongue confess that Jesus Christ is Lord" (Philippians 2:10-11). Whether they like it or not, everyone will one day have to admit that Christ is who He claimed to be.

📖 How does Christ going to the Father relate to the convicting work of the Holy Spirit in the area of righteousness?

While Christ was here on earth physically, He was the perfect manifestation of righteousness. Now that He is going to the Father, people need another way to understand what righteousness is. This is one of the ministries of the Spirit.

📖 Who is "the ruler of this world" and how does his being judged relate to the conviction of the Holy Spirit?

The "ruler of this world" (see also John 12:31) is Satan. Elsewhere we see him referred to as "the prince of the power of the air" (Ephesians 2:2), "the god of this age" (2 Corinthians 4:4), and "the evil one" in whose power the whole world lies (1 John 5:19). The Spirit convicts

PRACTICAL PRINCIPLES FOR A LIFE OF POWER

of judgment because Satan already stands as having been judged. He is simply awaiting the execution of his sentence. Since he is judged, then all who align themselves with him and his world system will also face judgment.

📖 What exactly was the problem with the disciples according to verse 12?

The basic idea is that they cannot understand now. The word "bear" points either to the weightiness of the information or the weakness of the disciples or both. The fact that He says "you cannot bear them now" points to the fact that at some point in the future (with the aid of the Spirit) they will be able to bear them.

📖 How does the Holy Spirit "guide us into all truth," and what specific areas do verses 13 and 15 relate this to?

The implication of the context (verse 12) is that the Holy Spirit will guide us into all the truth of God a little at a time as we are able to bear it. He is the Spirit of the sovereign God and His timing in our lives is perfect. Two specific areas of truth mentioned here are "what is to come" (Christ's death and resurrection as well as His second coming), and "all things that the Father has" (which points to the totality of doctrine). The doctrines recorded in the New Testament writings were disclosed to their authors by this revealing ministry of the Holy Spirit (see 2 Peter 1:20-21).

📖 What according to verse 14 is the result of this process?

Christ is glorified when the Spirit reveals truth to us.

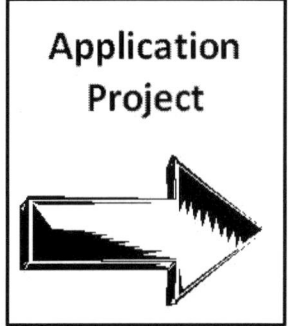

Application Project

"But I am afraid, lest as the serpent deceived Eve by his craftiness, that you should be led astray from the simplicity and purity of devotion to Christ"
- 2 Corinthians 11:3

One of the more uncomfortable promises of the Scriptures is found in 2 Timothy 3:12, "all who desire to live godly in Christ Jesus will be persecuted." Although I don't expect to see a line waiting to claim thisone, we really shouldn't be surprised when persecution comes. It is a logical consequence of walking with God in a world that is at war with Him. Conversely, we should be concerned if our faith encounters no opposition from the world. As someone once said, "if the world fits, your faith is the wrong size." When we encounter opposition, the key is to yield to the Spirit's control. He is able to convict the world, and He is the source of our strength, wisdom and direction. Jesus spoke these words to His disciples to keep them from stumbling. Consider the following as you seek to live a life of power in the face of persecution.

1. What opposition have you encountered as you seek to walk with God?

2. In what ways have you seen God work in your life through those situations?

3. In what ways have you seen God work through you in those situations?

4. Second Timothy 3:16 states "all Scripture is inspired by God and is profitable for TEACHING, for REPROOF, for CORRECTION, and for TRAINING IN RIGHTEOUSNESS." With that as an outline, consider the following for application:

A. TEACHING: What from this passage do I need to believe?

B. REPROOF: Is there any sin I need to confess?

C. CORRECTION: What do I need to do differently?

D. TRAINING IN RIGHTEOUSNESS: What is my main application point? (make it specific and measurable)

   Who is going to hold me accountable to this?

When am I going to do it? (put it in your schedule)

The most important thing in the Christian life is not what you know, but what you do with what you know (James 1:22, Luke 6:46).

Reminder:

John 14:15 states "if you love Me you will keep My commandments" and then in verses 16-17 Christ explains how we do that - ("and I will ask the Father, and He will give you another Helper...that is the Spirit..."). It is all-important that as we look at the applications God calls us to in His word, we recognize that we will only be able to accomplish those as we draw on the power of His Spirit indwelling us. Otherwise we will find ourselves trying to obey God through self-effort and we will ultimately fail. We see this necessity even in Christ. As John 14:10 puts it, "...the Father abiding in Me does His works." Why not take a moment to pray about this and give it to the Lord.

LESSON SIX

"Radical Christians Face a Radical Prospect: Eternity"

John 16:16-33

Full Fellowship With God (16:16-22)

📖 Why did the phrase "a little while" cause the disciples such confusion, and what is the timing Christ is referring to?

The phrase "a little while" appears 11 times in John's gospel, 9 of them in this discourse. The disciples' confusion makes it clear that they still do not understand He is to die as a sacrifice for sin. They are looking for the conquering lion of Judah who will set up the kingdom of God on earth, not the sacrifice lamb who's kingdom begins in the heart. The time Christ refers to is eternity. We become citizens of eternity the moment we place our trust in Christ. Eternity begins for us at that point.

📖 How is the promise, "a little while, and you will see Me" significant, and how is that a blessing to us?

Whenever Jesus speaks of His coming it is always in imminent terms ("Behold, I am coming quickly"). One might argue that 2,000 years isn't very quick, but that isn't an accurate way to view it. Although Jesus didn't come back to earth in the disciples' lifetimes, He did come for them at the end of their lives. At the moment of death they saw Jesus. The sixty or seventy years of life are but a vapor when compared to eternity. As to how this promise is a blessing, the greatest blessing of heaven will be seeing Jesus face to face. In 1 John 3:2 we read, "...when He appears, we shall be like Him, because we shall see Him just as He is." Seeing Jesus is a transforming event. The flip side of this truth is that no matter how great our concept of God is, it is inadequate and incomplete, for we have not yet truly seen Him "just as He is." All the other glories of heaven combined will pale in comparison to the wonder of seeing Him.

📖 Break down Christ's answer in verse 20 to their question, and identify what each part refers to.

In verse 20 Christ relates that upon His death (the timing of "you will not behold Me"), the disciples will weep and lament while the world rejoices. They will be sorrowful, but "when they see Him again" their sorrow will turn to joy. The word "lament" here refers to the loud wailing and lamentation that is the customary reaction to death in the Middle East.

📖 Why doesn't Christ answer their question directly, and where does His answer force them to place their trust?

PRACTICAL PRINCIPLES FOR A LIFE OF POWER

Christ doesn't give them anywhere to hang their trust except to take Him at His word. This is the essence of what faith is. It is not trying to believe something hard enough so as to make it come true, it is simply taking God at His word that He will do what He has said or that what He has said will come to pass.

📖 What is significant about Christ's return being compared to a woman giving birth and where else is this analogy used?

The childbirth analogy is the strongest point against the idea that Christ is referring simply to their joy at the resurrection. In Matthew 24:8, Mark 13:8, 1 Thessalonians 5:3, and Revelation 12 we see the idea of childbirth applied to the 2nd coming of Christ. Matthew refers to Christ's coming as being similar to the birth pangs of a woman. In other words, the signs before His coming will increase in intensity just as the pains of a woman in labor.

📖 How is the promise of verse 22 a blessing to us?

While this promise is partially fulfilled in the post-resurrection appearances (which certainly caused joy, though not unending joy), their complete fulfillment is only in eternity, for it isn't until then that every tear is wiped away. What a blessing to have joy that never fades nor fails. We experience glimpses of this now, but when He returns there will no longer be the pains and failures and trials that sometimes steal our joy here.

Full Knowledge Of God (16:23-30)

📖 To what "day" is Christ referring here, and what is the blessing to the believer in this verse?

That the "day" referred to here is at some point after their conversation is clear. The question is, does the "day" refer to the resurrection or the second coming. Probably the best answer is "both." While it is partially fulfilled after the resurrection, it is not completely fulfilled until heaven. The blessing we speak of is having all our questions answered. Notice Christ's words at the beginning: "in that day you will ask me no question."

📖 What are the parameters and context of the promise in verse 24, and how should this be applied?

While this promise is similar to the one in 14:13-14, the context is not asking for possessions or provision, but asking questions. Again we see that this promise, though partially fulfilled now, will find its fruition in eternity. Then we will have the full joy (perfect tense - complete) of being able to ask anything of the Father.

📖 What are the parameters of our understanding of the spiritual truths spoken of here, and what will they be "in that day?"

Verse 25 reiterates the fact that our understanding of spiritual truth requires analogy and figurative language now, but in eternity we will be taught plainly. This promise is reminiscent of 1 Corinthians 13:9-12 which teaches, "...we know in part and we prophesy in part; for when the perfect comes, the partial will be done away...for now we see in a mirror dimly, but then face to face; now I know in part, but then I shall know fully."

📖 What does it mean to "ask in My name" and why do we pray that way?

Asking in Jesus' name is much more than a spiritual way of saying "the end" at the finish of a prayer. In one sense, it means to pray in accord with the desires and will of Christ, as though we were acting on His behalf. It also includes the truth that the Father hears our prayers because of Christ's righteousness, not our own. We enter His presence always and only by the finished work of Christ. When we pray that way, we are recognizing that truth and reminding ourselves of it.

📖 Why will God answer their (and our) prayers according to verses 26-27, and how is this a blessing?

The truth here, a tremendous one, is that which is expressed in Hebrews 10:19, "...we have confidence to enter the holy place by the blood of Jesus." In Old Testament times the High Priest alone could enter the holy place and then only once a year on "Yom Kippur" (the day of atonement when he would sprinkle sacrificial blood on the altar to cover the sins of the nation). While in the holy place there would be a rope around the High Priest's ankle and bells on the fringe of his robe. So long as the bells jingled the attendants knew all was well, for if the priest were not ceremonially pure and acceptable before God he would be struck dead. The rope was to provide a means of dragging him out, for no one else could go in there. This was the old way, but when Jesus died on the cross, the veil of the holy place was torn in two, picturing the opening of the presence of God to all who come by the blood of His lamb. Now we can boldly enter the presence of God without fear because of the completed work of Christ.

📖 What is the significance of verse 28 in this context?

Remember that in 14:3 Jesus told them that His going to the Father included the promise that He would come for them. This statement is a reminder that earth is no longer home for us, just as it was never really home for Christ. We must keep eternity in focus so that we don't cling too tightly to this present world. If the world fits then our faith is the wrong size.

📖 What was the response of the disciples and why did they respond that way?

The disciples' response is that finally they are getting the picture. He is getting through to them. As for why they responded that way, it took Jesus spelling things out –"I...AM...GOING...TO...THE...FATHER" – for them to get the message.

📖 What was the result of the disciples' understanding, and how did they discern that Christ didn't have to be asked questions (see verse 19)?

As a result of the disciples finally getting the picture, they drew the conclusion that Jesus knew all things. If you look at this verse by itself this doesn't make sense, but when you put it in its context you see from verse 19 that Jesus answers their question without them asking it. From this they are beginning to recognize Christ's omniscience, and the result is that they believed He came from God.

Full Victory In God (16:31-33)

📖 What was Christ's reason for asking if the disciples now believed; was this a rebuke or a concern?

Perhaps a bit of both, but mainly concern. It is as if Jesus is saying, "You better believe, for that belief will soon be tested, and in a way you do not expect."

📖 What is the "hour" spoken of here and how does it relate to the question of verse 31?

The "hour" spoken of here is the time of culmination of the earthly ministry of Christ, namely, the crucifixion. If refers not to a literal hour but to a span of time. Jesus began speaking of His "hour" at the beginning of His earthly ministry at the wedding in Cana (2:4). His hour has now come and He is about to be crucified. That is why He asked the disciples if they really believed.

📖 What is significant about Christ not being alone, and how does that relate to us?

The statement, "...and to leave Me alone; and yet I am not alone, because the Father is with Me" is an awesome truth. Even when Christ was abandoned by all His earthly companions and friends, He was not alone. The Father was with Him. This truth is a promise to us as well, for in Hebrews 13:5 Christ promises "I will never leave you nor forsake you."

📖 What does the "these things" of verse 33 refer to and what is the resulting blessing to us?

The statement "these things" refers not to the immediately preceding words, but to the entirety of His conversation with them this evening. The "Upper Room Discourse" is now officially at an end. Chapter 17 records the subsequent prayer of Christ for His disciples. The blessing here is that though not in their circumstances (for scattering, persecution and the crucifixion of their master awaited them) but in their Lord they would find peace. This is a blessing to us as well, for in Ephesians 2:14 we read, "He Himself is our peace."

📖 What is the blessing to us in the last part of verse 33, and how did Christ overcome the world?

The blessing to Christ's disciples (both past and present) is that although they will find persecution in the world, Jesus has overcome the world. The word "overcome" has as its root the Greek word NIKE (from which the tennis shoes derive their name) which means "to conquer, or to be victorious." Christ overcame the world when, by the sacrifice of Himself, He released us from its chains. It is a prophetic promise of the future victory that awaits us in eternity. All the world can do is kill the body, but our eternal destiny is secure.

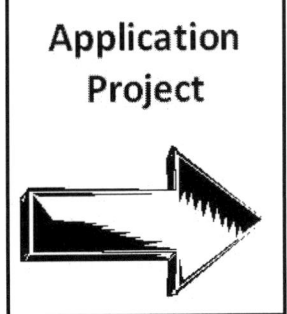

Application Project ➡

"But I am afraid, lest as the serpent deceived Eve by his craftiness, your minds should be led stray from the simplicity and purity of devotion to Christ"
- 2 Corinthians 11:3

If a Christian accurately understands the realities of heaven and eternity, it will radically alter the choices he makes and the way he lives his life. An "eternal perspective" is an essential to living life God's way and it requires regular maintenance to keep in place. The joys of heaven as they are detailed here, should when kept in view, keep us from misplaced priorities. As Paul exhorts in Colossians 3:2, "set your minds on the things above, not on the things of the earth."

Conversely, a mind set on the things of earth will cause us to devalue the things of God and the true riches of heaven. As Christ looked to the cross and prepared to pass the torch of His ministry to His disciples, He paused to remind them of eternity. Certainly if we seek to serve Him we must take that reminder to heart. Consider the following as you seek to keep eternity in focus.

1. In what ways have you experienced success in keeping an eternal perspective and what were the results of it in your walk?

2. What are some examples from your past experience of the consequences of not operating from an eternal perspective?

3. What are some present areas of your walk with God that reflect adeficiency in your eternal perspective?

4. How well versed are you on the Biblical teaching about what heaven is like?

5. Second Timothy 3:16 states "all Scripture is inspired by God and is profitable for TEACHING, for REPROOF, for CORRECTION, and for TRAINING IN RIGHTEOUSNESS." With that as an outline, consider the following for application:

A. TEACHING: What from this passage do I need to believe?

B. REPROOF: Is there any sin I need to confess?

C. CORRECTION: What do I need to do differently?

D. TRAINING IN RIGHTEOUSNESS: What is my main application point? (make it specific and measurable)

Who is going to hold me accountable to this?

When am I going to do it? (put it in your schedule)

The most important thing in the Christian life is not what you know, but what you do with what you know (James 1:22, Luke 6:46).

Reminder:
John 14:15 states "if you love Me you will keep My commandments" and then in verses 16-17 Christ explains how we do that - ("and I will ask the Father, and He will give you another Helper...that is the Spirit..."). It is all-important that as we look at the applications God calls us to in His word, we recognize that we will only be able to accomplish those as we draw on the power of His Spirit indwelling us. Otherwise we will find ourselves trying to obey God through self-effort and we will ultimately fail. We see this necessity even in Christ. As John 14:10 puts it, "...the Father abiding in Me does His works." Why not take a moment to pray about this and give it to the Lord.

LESSON SEVEN

"RADICAL CHRISTIANS ARE THE RESULT OF A RADICAL PRAYER"

John 17:1-26

That God's Glory Would Be Multiplied

📖 Find out what the word "glorify" means, and identify and categorize each time it is used in this chapter.

The Greek word translated "glorify" means "to render conspicuous and glorious the divine character and attributes of God." The root word appears eight times in this chapter – 17:1 (twice), 17:4, 17:5 (twice), 17:10, 17:22, and 17:24. It is also implied in verse 5 ("together with Thyself"), and verse 22 ("I have given to them" i.e. disciples). The idea is used once of the Son giving glory to the disciples (verse 22), once of the glory the Son has (verse 5), once of the glory the Father has (verse 5), once of the Father glorifying Himself (verse 5), and twice of the Son glorifying the Father (verses 1, 4). The majority of the references though are of the Father glorifying the Son (verses 1, 5, 10, 22, and 24).

📖 How would the Father glorify Christ, and in what future ways would Christ glorify the Father?

The Father brings glory to Christ when He reveals to others who Christ is (most clearly through the resurrection). In Jesus' prayer He is revealing that the time has come for the world to recognize Him for who He really is. This is partially fulfilled through the resurrection, but will be ultimately and completely fulfilled at his second coming when every knee shall bow and every tongue confess that Jesus Christ is Lord. The Father is glorified through Christ by His obedience and work. His obedience leads Him to the cross (Philippians 2:8).

📖 What exactly is Christ's authority mentioned in verse 2, and how does this relate to verse 1?

The Father has given the Son authority to give eternal life to all the Father has given Him. In other words, the Father gave to the Son those who would believe, and He also gave the Son the authority to give eternal life to them. The word "give" appears in 3 forms here: 1) The Father "gave" authority, 2) all whom God has "given" Him, and 3) He may "give" eternal life. The first and last of these are in the "aorist tense" meaning a simple action at a point in time. The 2nd however, is in the "perfect tense" and the meaning of this is significant. The perfect tense indicates that those given by the Father to the Son are given permanently. It points to the perfection of salvation and that those who believe are eternally secure. This all relates to verse 1 in that both the Father and the Son are glorified through our eternal salvation.

📖 We generally view eternal life quantitatively, but here the emphasis seems to be qualitative. How does verse 3 define eternal life, and for what purpose was Christ "sent"?

Verse 3 shows us that the primary purpose of eternal life is not living in a mansion, living forever, walking streets of gold, or avoiding the fires of hell. The main purpose of eternal life is to know God, and to know His Son. The word "know" is in the "present tense" meaning that eternal life is for us to continue to "know" Him, progressive, continuous knowledge. Because of this, we don't have to wait until heaven to begin experiencing eternal life. Paul wrote in Philippians 3 (some 25-30 years after his conversion) that he counted all things to be loss compared to knowing Christ. It is noteworthy that there are two Greek words for "life", *bios* and *zoe*. *Bios* (from which we derive our English word "biology") means existence, live as opposed to dead. This kind of life encompasses everything from amoebae to man. *zoe* on the other hand (from which we derive our English word "zoology") is a narrower term. Just as zoology doesn't include all life forms, but only the higher forms from the animal kingdom, *zoe* doesn't mean life as mere existence, but life in its essence, the quality of life. It means to "really live, not just to exist." It is *zoe* that is used here in this reference to eternal life. Jesus was "sent" for this very purpose. As John 10:10 puts it, "I come that they might have life, and might have it abundantly." In other words, He came not to bring mere existence (*bios*), but to bring life in all its fullness (*zoe*).

📖 How according to verse 4 did Christ glorify God, and how does this relate to us?

Christ brought glory to the Father by accomplishing the work the Father gave Him to do. In the same way, we glorify God as we serve Him and follow His leading. It is important to mention that the word "work" here appears in the Greek with the definite article placing special emphasis on the word "the." In other words, "...having accomplished THE work..." The point is, we don't glorify God simply by going out and working hard for Him. We bring glory to the Father as we seek His will and involve ourselves in the specific work He calls us to. We first need to hear from Him, and then our work will be following His leading.

PRACTICAL PRINCIPLES FOR A LIFE OF POWER

📖 Christ mentions in verse 5 the work the Father "gave Him" to do. Look through the chapter and identify everything the Father "gave" the Son.

The Father "gave" the Son authority to give eternal life (verse 2), The Father has "given" Jesus work to do (verse 4), He "gave" Jesus His disciples (verse 6 – twice, verses 9, 24), 17:7 speaks of everything Thou hast given Me". The Father "gave" Jesus the words to speak (verse 8), He has "given" Jesus His "name" (verses 11,12), and He has "given " Jesus glory (verses 22,24).

📖 Break down verse 5 and write your observations.

In verse 5 Jesus is asking the Father to glorify the Son and Himself, and Jesus clarifies that He is asking the Father for the glory He had before the incarnation. This points to the eternality of Christ in that He existed before the world. It also shows us that Jesus' eternal glory has been interrupted only by His obedient choice to come to earth (Philippians 2:5-11).

📖 Observe verses 6-8 and identify how Christ "manifested" the Father and what the response was with the disciples.

The answer to this question is in the last phrase of verse 6: "and they have kept Thy word." We see in John 1:1 that you can't separate God from His word. When Jesus gave to the disciples the words the Father had given Him (verse 8), He was revealing the Father to them. John 1:14 explains that Jesus Himself is the God/man, the word that "became flesh, and dwelt among us", and that as "we beheld His glory" we were able to recognize that He was from the Father. John 1:18 puts it this way: "No man has seen God at any time...He has explained Him." In verses 7-8 we see that the disciples responded to Christ's manifesting the Father by "receiving" Jesus' words, by "truly understanding", and by "believing" the Father had sent Him.

📖 Identify every time the word "world" appears in this chapter and its usual use.

The word "world" appears 18 times in this chapter: verse 5, verse 6, verse 9, verse 11 (twice), verse 13, verse 14 (3 times), verse 15, verse 16 (twice), verse 18 (twice), verse 21, verse 23, verse 24, and verse 25. It almost always refers not to the physical world, but to the world as that system that is not aligned with God and does not know Him (verse 25). We see that the disciples were called out of this system (verse 6), but that though they no longer serve this world system (they are not "of" it – verses 14, 16), they still live in it (verse 11), and this by the will of God (verse 15). We also see that this world system hates the followers of God (verse 14), that Jesus was "sent" to this same world (verse 18), and that Jesus, in turn, sent His disciples to reach out to this same rebellious world (verse 18), so that the world might believe (verses 21, 23).

📖 Identify exactly what Christ is praying for in verses 9-10 and how this relates to us.

Christ is praying "on behalf of" the disciples. He is not just interested in them as laborers, but is seeking their welfare. Christ is also seeking that God's glory would be multiplied in Christ and through Him in the disciples. This prayer reaches all the way to us, for it is the will of the Father and the Son that God would be glorified in us.

That God's Ministry Would Be Multiplied

📖 What exactly does Christ pray for in verse 11, and what does this reveal about the disciples' needs?

The bottom line of Christ's request is that the disciples would be one with He and the Father. Christ doesn't desire just unity, but that the disciples would be unified around the Lord. He does not desire the kind of man-centered unity that sacrifices truth for the sake of agreement. Instead, He is seeking the unity that flows from surrender to God. In the context of Christ's prayer, we must recognize that during His earthly ministry, it was easy for the disciples to be unified around Him, for He was always with them. Now that He is "no more in the world" (verse 11), it would be through their cooperation with the Spirit that unity would be achieved.

📖 What is significant about God's name as Christ refers to here? In the Greek construction here, the term translated "in" (*en*) is both local and instrumental. They are both to be marked with and protected by the divine name. The name of God throughout Scripture is revelatory of His nature and character. Notice the term "keep" here. We are "kept" by the Father (verse 11), the Son (verse 12), and presumable the attending work of the Spirit which Christ previously discussed with the disciples. Notice that we are not kept by our own striving and faithfulness. The disciples were kept first by Christ's personal involvement in their lives as the good shepherd (John 10), and now by His constant intercession (Hebrews 7:24-25). The same is true for us. It was the Father who began this work in us, and He will perfect it until our Lord's return (Philippians 1:6).

📖 What does "son of perdition" mean, who is it referring to, and what Scripture does it fulfill?

The term "perdition" means destruction or damnation, one destined to perish. The reference is obviously to Judas, whose betrayal was prophesied in Psalm 41:9. That he was not saved is evident here. Christ's wording is a play on words: "none of them perished, but the son of perishing".

📖 What are the "these things" Christ speaks, and how do they fit in with joy?

The "these things" Christ speaks here refer not just to His prayer, but to the entirety of the message He has communicated to the disciples this night. The all-important truth here is that our joy is in our relationship with the Lord, not in our circumstances. Because of this, it is possible for us to continue in this joy even though the world may hate us and we may walk in the same persecution the disciples encountered.

📖 Identify from verses 14-17 all the results of us getting God's Word and the ramifications of this toward ministry.

The "word" (not just Scripture, but our obedience to Scripture) brings first, persecution (verse 14). Paul wrote to Timothy, "all who desire to live godly in Christ Jesus will be persecuted" (2 Timothy 3:12). The world hates those who follow God, because by our life and choices we aren't "of" the world. If the world fits then something is wrong with our faith. Second, our obedience to the word brings protection (verse 15). We see this implied in Jesus' words in verse 15. We see here that Jesus doesn't want to take us out of the world (for that is where our ministry is), but to keep us from the evil one. We are protected from the world as we are obedient to God. Third, our obedience to the word bring peculiarity (verse 16). We will be different from the world if we follow God. First Peter 1:1 identifies us as "aliens". Fourth, our obedience to the word brings purity (verse 17). We see here that truth brings sanctification (Christ-likeness). Obviously this elevates the importance of the word in our ministry, for if our ministry is not Scripture-based and Scripture-focused it will not impart changed lives. It is the word of God that equips us for the work of God (2 Timothy 3:17).

📖 Why does Christ not ask the Father to take the disciples out of the world, and how does this relate to us?

This is very significant, for there always is a tendency for believers to wall themselves off from the world by only having Christian friends and having all our activities "Christianized" (e.g. "Christian Skate Night"). But the reality is, God does not want us out of the world. If He did, then we would go immediately to heaven as soon as we were saved. What God wants is to get the world out of us, but to leave us in the world so that we might be His ambassadors there (2 Corinthians 5).

📖 How does Christ's example relate to His sending of the disciples, and how does sanctification fit in with this?

The main point of verse 19 is that Christ's followers are to take up the task that He Himself was committed to: "to seek and to save the lost." As for sanctification, the word means, "to set apart for God and His holy purposes." The more we become like Christ in character, the more we become like Him in purpose. Remember, Jesus said, "follow Me and I will make you fishers of men." If we aren't fishing, we aren't following.

📖 How does Christ's prayer change in verse 20 and what exactly is He asking for?

In verse 20 Jesus shifts His focus from His eleven disciples, to all who would believe as a result of their ministry. That includes us. What Jesus is praying is that like the disciples, we too would be in the world but not of it, and we too would be sent of Him into the world (verse 18). This is what the Great Commission (Matthew 28:18-20) is all about.

📖 How according to verses 21-23 does unity relate to ministry and where does unity come from?

In order for us to be a part of God's work, we must be one with Him. Unless you read this passage carefully, you might draw the wrong conclusion that Jesus is praying the disciples will be one with each other, but notice verse 21: "...that they may be in Us." Jesus is saying that just as He is one with the Father, the disciples must be one with He and the Father. In Ephesians 4:3 we read, "being diligent to preserve the unity of the Spirit." First, unity is "of the Spirit." In other words, since there is only one Spirit, if He is ruling and reigning in the hearts of believers, unity is automatic, for the Spirit does not war against Himself. Second, unity is to be preserved, not produced. Trying to unify believers is a futile effort, for the only way unity may be achieved is as all parties are surrendered to the Lord.

📖 What is the significance of Christ being in us and us being in the world?

The result of Christ being in us, and us being in the world, is that Christ is still in the world in us. This is incarnational evangelism: Christ in me in the world. As I yield myself to Christ and He is manifested in Me, the world is able to see the reality of Christ in me. The result of this kind of oneness with the Lord is "that the world my believe...".

📖 Compare and contrast the statements of verse 24 with verse 15 and 20, writing your observations.

Verse 15 makes it clear that Christ is not asking the Father to take us out of the world, yet in verse 24 it is also clear that Christ desires that we be with Him. The answer to this seeming contradiction is in verse 20 where we see that the only reason we are not with the Lord now is because of our mission: those who will believe through us.

📖 What according to verses 24-26 are the promised results to believers?

When we are finally with Christ, we will a) behold His glory – verse 24 (1 John 3:2 speaks of seeing Him as He really is), b) we will "know" and understand the Father (verses 25-26), and c) we will experience the love of God (verse 26).

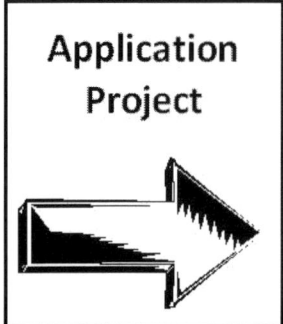

Application Project

"But I am afraid, lest as the serpent deceived Eve by his craftiness, your minds should be led astray from the simplicity and purity of devotion to Christ"
- 2 Corinthians 11:3

If anyone knows how prayer works it is our Lord Jesus Christ. Here in John 17, what is known as the "High Priestly Prayer." we can learn much by His example. It should be noted that more important than the content alone is the fact that Christ prayed. This may seem a bit obvious, but in its simplicity it is easy to stumble over.If Christ expressed His dependence on God through prayer, so should we. This is not to say that prayer is something mystical in itself. Prayer has no intrinsic power. It is only powerful because God is powerful. He is not so concerned with the formulas as He is with the heart of faith behind it. As we look at the prayer of Christ we can see the kind of things we need to be trusting God for and we can see the heart attitude He desires. Consider the following applications as you pursue a more radical Christianity.

1. Take a moment to remind yourself of some of the significant prayers you have seen God answer.

2. What is most dissatisfying about your present experiences with prayer?

3. Second Timothy 3:16 states "all Scripture is inspired by God and is profitable for TEACHING, for REPROOF, for CORRECTION, and for TRAINING IN RIGHTEOUSNESS." With that as an outline, consider the following for application:

A. TEACHING: What from this passage do I need to believe?

B. REPROOF: Is there any sin I need to confess?

C. CORRECTION: What do I need to do differently?

D. TRAINING IN RIGHTEOUSNESS: What is my main application point? (make it specific and measurable)

Who is going to hold me accountable to this?

When am I going to do it? (put it in your schedule)

The most important thing in the Christian life is not what you know, but what you do with what you know (James 1:22, Luke 6:46).

Reminder:

John 14:15 states "if you love Me you will keep My commandments" and then in verses 16-17 Christ explains how we do that - ("and I will ask the Father, and He will give you another Helper...that is the Spirit..."). It is all-important that as we look at the applications God calls us to in His word, we recognize that we will only be able to accomplish those as we draw on the power of His Spirit indwelling us. Otherwise we will find ourselves trying to obey God through self-effort and we will ultimately fail. We see this necessity even in Christ. As John 14:10 puts it, "...the Father abiding in Me does His works." Why not take a moment to pray about this and give it to the Lord.

ABOUT THE AUTHOR

Eddie Rasnake graduated with honors from East Tennessee State University. He and his wife, Michele, served 7 years with Cru at UVa, James Madison, and as campus director at the University of Tennessee. Eddie left Cru to join Wayne Barber at Woodland Park Baptist Church where he still serves as Senior Associate Pastor. He has authored dozens of books and Bible studies and has published materials in Afrikaans, Albanian, German, Greek, Italian, Romanian, Russian and Telugu. Eddie and his wife Michele live in Chattanooga, Tennessee.

What Christian Leaders have to say about Eddie Rasnake's books:

"I encourage you to make these studies a part of your study of God's Word - I am confident you will be blessed!" – **Dr. Bill Bright**, Founder of Cru

"If you long to understand how God dynamically works in the lives of people like you and me, 'Following God' will be food for your soul." – **John MacArthur**, Pastor-Teacher, Grace Community Church

"These three dear men who love God and love His Word have produced an excellent study that will help you see in real life, flesh and blood examples, the cruciality of 'Following God' fully." – **Kay Arthur**, Executive Director, Precept Ministries International

"A wonderful resource for those who are serious in their Bible Study." – **Adrian Rogers**, Pastor, Bellevue Baptist Church, Memphis, Tennessee

"This study consistently takes the student to the Word of God. A refreshing study that stays true to scripture." – **Henry T. Blackaby**, co-author of Experiencing God

"Throughout my ministry of forty-one years, I have never read anything more fresh and enlightening than this book of knowing and living the will of God." – **Reverend Bill Stafford**, Evangelist, Director, International Congress on Revival

"I highly recommend this book not only to the new believer...but also to the older saint who would like a fresh look at how to discover God's will." – **Jan Silvious**, Author and Speaker

"You won't regret the time you spend reading Eddie Rasnake's book. I count it a privilege to know him personally and work with him. His book will help you read the signposts of decisions correctly and properly." – **Dr. Spiros Zodhiates**, Editor of The Hebrew/Greek Key Study Bible, President Emeritus, AMG International.

"If your heart's desire is to become a devoted follower of Christ, then 'Following God' will serve as a compelling roadmap." – **Joseph Stowell**, President Emeritus, Moody Bible Institute

"Fresh, original, imaginative – and Biblical – were the words that came to mind as I read 'What Should I Do, Lord?' Easy reading makes the principles accessible even to the newest Christian." – **Ron Dunn**, Author and Speaker

"Those who seek to do God's will often make decisions with lifelong impact. The tendency is to want to see our names written in the sky along with specific instructions as to what to do. Eddie Rasnake helps young and old alike understand how to know God's will by seeking God's way." – **Frank Brock**, President Emeritus, Covenant College

Printed in Great Britain
by Amazon